VOCABULARY 5

FOR YOUNG CATHOLICS

WRITTEN BY
SETON STAFF

SETON PRESS
FRONT ROYAL, VA

Executive Editor: Dr. Mary Kay Clark
Editors: Seton Staff
Illustrator: Benjamin Hatke

Seton Home Study School
1350 Progress Drive
Front Royal, VA 22630
540-636-9990
540-636-1602 fax

ISBN: 978-1-60704-060-6

For more information, visit us on the Web at http://www.setonhome.org.
Contact us by e-mail at info@setonhome.org.

Cover: *Jesus Amongst the Doctors,* Jean Auguste Dominique Ingres

DEDICATED TO THE SACRED HEART OF JESUS

VOCABULARY 5 FOR YOUNG CATHOLICS

CONTENTS

Introduction: Notes for Parents vii

Lesson 1: Say What You Mean 1

Lesson 2: Matt and the Large Ox 5

Lesson 3: Parts of a Book. 9

Lesson 4: Aunt Sarah's Duck 13

Lesson 5: Ough - Ouch! 17

Lesson 6: Connections 21

Lesson 7: A Turning Point. 25

Lesson 8: The Seed Project 29

Lesson 9: Moving Along 33

Lesson 10: The Porpoise with a Purpose 37

Lesson 11: The All Day Two-Hour Trip 41

Lesson 12: Here Comes Trouble 45

Lesson 13: A Simple Watermelon Seed 49

Lesson 14: Guess Who? 53

Lesson 15: Silly Milly 57

Lesson 16: Let the Show Begin 61

Lesson 17: What Shall We Call the Baby? 65

Lesson 18: Uncle Ronald Had a Farm 69

Lesson 19: E - I - E - I - Oh - Oh .73

Lesson 20: Making a Memory 77

Lesson 21: Limericks Are Fun 81

Lesson 22: Meet the Smiths. 85

Lesson 23: The Pledge of Allegiance 89

Lesson 24: Good Job, Zoe 93

Answer Key 97

Alphabetical Listing of Words 103

NOTES FOR PARENTS

Preface

It is important for students to learn new words as well as different meanings of words they already know. It is also important for students to remember the new vocabulary words and definitions and to apply them in their speaking and writing. In this grade level, students are writing answers to specific questions as well as writing sentences in their other courses, and the vocabulary words studied in this book will enhance those assignments.

With the beginning reading selection in each lesson, our purpose is to motivate students to want to learn new vocabulary words or different meanings of words. The beginning reading selection is meant to be fun and entertaining. The reading usually contains a playful twist that incorporates fifteen vocabulary words. Not only are the reading selections fun to read, but they are purposeful. Students are more apt to learn vocabulary words when they see them in the context of sentences, or in the context of an entertaining story.

Besides learning new words, or different meanings for words, students need to practice using words so they remember them over time. Repetition helps memorization. You will notice we have several exercises: looking up the words in a dictionary, identifying words in a list, comparing similar words and contrasting opposite words, using words in sentences, identifying words for a crossword puzzle, and an optional exercise using the thesaurus to find synonyms and antonyms. Seton sells the *Merriam-Webster's Intermediate Thesaurus*.

We believe students will become familiar with these words and comfortable enough with the words to use them in their speech and writing. Seton encourages you, the parent, to think about using these words in daily conversation, especially during the week your student is studying these words.

Notice that sometimes we use a word, such as an adjective, but the main entry in the dictionary will be a noun. In most cases, the adjective is included in the dictionary citation under the noun form of the word. We <u>usually use the form of the word in the list of words in the same part of speech used in the reading selection, but sometimes we use the main form of the word, such as the infinitive form of a verb instead of a past tense. The sentence exercise usually uses the same form as in the main list of words.</u>

Lesson Contents

Reading Selection: This is a simple, usually entertaining story that incorporates practical vocabulary words. The story appeals to students, and the words make sense to them.

Exercise A: This is a list of vocabulary words and their part of speech. Students learn to look up words in the dictionary, to pronounce them correctly, and to locate the definition which is appropriate for the particular use in the reading selection.

Exercise B: This is a list of words usually related to a specified situation. This exercise is aimed to help the student see that the meaning of a word can often be determined through a relationship.

Exercise C: These are word groups that further comprehension. The student must think about each word's meaning and match the two words that have either similar meanings or opposite meanings.
An optional thesaurus exercise is also suggested. As the student uses a thesaurus, he further expands his vocabulary as he learns synonyms and antonyms for the lesson's vocabulary words.

Exercise D: These are sentences that require students to remember and to apply the words they have learned in the lesson. Most of these sentences are related to the Catholic Faith or Catholic life, following the directives of the Vatican regarding Catholic schools and textbooks used in Catholic schools.

Crossword Puzzle: This is a popular exercise with students. This exercise is an enjoyable and rewarding way to recall the words they have used.

Answer Key: Located in the back of the book, the key contains answers for Exercises B, C, and D of each lesson.

Suggested Procedure

Notice that there are six lessons per quarter. A quarter review test may be given at any time during the seventh, eighth, or ninth week of the quarter. Seton's lesson plans include a quarter review test.

We encourage parents to give a weekly quiz, the parent giving the definition and asking the student to write out the correct vocabulary word. Seton's lesson plans include weekly quizzes.

Each lesson may be completed within one week. It is up to the parent to determine whether the student should cover the exercises in three, four, or five days. Keep in mind that review, repetition, and application over several days is more easily retained in the memory.

Approach 1: Complete one lesson in a week. First, the student reads the reading selection and then underlines in the reading the vocabulary words from the list in Exercise A. During the week, complete Exercises A through D and the Crossword Puzzle. At the end of the week, the student takes a weekly quiz administered and graded by the parent. There are six lessons for each quarter.

Approach 2: Complete one lesson in a week. First, the student reads the reading selection and then underlines in the reading the vocabulary words from the list in Exercise A. Next, complete the Crossword Puzzle. Students love crossword puzzles. However, students should not copy the definitions for the puzzle in writing the definitions for Exercise A, primarily because students need to practice using the dictionary. During the remainder of the week, complete Exercises A through D.

At the end of the week, the student takes a weekly quiz administered and graded by the parent. There are six lessons for each quarter.

Continuous Development: This vocabulary book provides your child a method to learn new vocabulary words. Whenever he encounters an unfamiliar word in his leisure or academic readings, he will know to examine the word within the context of the reading, and to locate it in a dictionary for pronunciation and its appropriate definition. Since this book has six lessons for each nine-week quarter, the student may devote the extra time to his other courses or enjoy leisure reading. Time devoted to leisure reading will continue to expand your child's vocabulary far beyond the words studied in these lessons.

Using the Dictionary and Thesaurus

There are vitally important lessons to be learned in using a dictionary: reviewing alphabetical order past the 1st, 2nd, or 3rd letter; using the Guide Words to locate words; noticing the Guide Words after finding the word; reading and discovering the different meanings one word can have; discovering the different parts of speech for a single word. For the majority of words in this book, words can be found in a children's dictionary. However, be alert and look for other forms of the word if necessary. For example, the word *nippy* is contained in one of these lessons; some dictionaries contain only *nip*; some dictionaries contain only *nippy*; some dictionaries contain both.

We encourage students to use a thesaurus. A thesaurus contains numerous synonyms, each having its own distinct meaning. When your student does any writing, encourage him or her to use a "new" word from the thesaurus. See if you can help your child to understand the small differences in synonyms. An optional thesaurus exercise is suggested in Exercise C. Encourage your student to use words or encourage your child to think about different words as you speak together throughout the day. This develops analytical skills to a high degree.

LESSON 1

SAY WHAT YOU MEAN

In this course, you will learn a method to help you master vocabulary words. First, look up an unfamiliar word in the dictionary. Remember that a word may have multiple meanings. Be sure to distinguish the differences. Second, determine the meaning that pertains to a particular sentence. Next, write a sentence and insert the new word in a suitable way. Do not hesitate to use new vocabulary words in your own writing. Use them with confidence in your speaking. If you choose accurate words to say precisely what you mean, your compositions will be more effective. We urge you to apply this method, not only to English, but to all subjects. Most of all, have fun with your new words!

EXERCISE A In the reading above, underline the words (or form of the words) that appear in the list below. Write the dictionary definition for the specific part of speech (noun, verb, adjective, or adverb) as used in the reading.

1. method (n.) _____

2. master (v.) _____

3. unfamiliar (adj.) _____

4. multiple (adj.) _____

5. distinguish (v.) _____

6. determine (v.) _____

7. pertain (v.) _____

8. insert (v.) _____

9. hesitate (v.) _____

10. confidence (n.) _____

11. accurate (adj.) _____

12. precisely (adv.) _____

13. effective (adj.) _____

14. urge (v.) _____

15. apply (v.) _____

EXERCISE B

Circle the correct word.

1. Which word means *to tell the difference* between a daisy and a rose?

    a) **distinguish**   b) **pertain**   c) **apply**   d) **hesitate**

2. Which word means our words say *exactly* what we mean?

    a) **unfamiliar**   b) **multiple**   c) **accurate**   d) **master**

3. Which word relates to adding something to a list?

    a) **determine**   b) **urge**   c) **distinguish**   d) **insert**

4. Which word relates to pausing a bit before deciding to walk up to someone?

    a) **unfamiliar**   b) **hesitate**   c) **pertain**   d) **effective**

5. Which word means to use great skills with tools?

    a) **compose**   b) **master**   c) **determine**   d) **apply**

EXERCISE C

Circle two words which either are similar or opposite meanings. Write the letter **S** if they are similar, or **O** if they are opposite. *Optional:* Use a thesaurus for more synonyms and antonyms for Exercise A words.

1. confidence   method   doubt   vocabulary   _____

2. apply   exactly   precisely   very   _____

3. multiple   effective   unfamiliar   strange   _____

4. distinguish   urge   pertain   discourage   _____

5. accurate   unknown   multiple   single   _____

EXERCISE D   Write on the line the correct list word to complete each sentence.

Mom encouraged Bob to have _ in learning the Mass responses.	1. _____
Johnny admitted he was _ with the story of St. George.	2. _____
Sally thought the questions did not _ to the main idea of the book.	3. _____
Father Bailey will _ the teens to join the pro-life organization.	4. _____
_ the shortest route to St. Anne's Church.	5. _____
Monica did not _ to help the children cross the street.	6. _____
Dad said to return at _ three o'clock.	7. _____
Mom's _ for making pancakes cannot be beat!	8. _____
St. John Bosco was _ in helping the boys learn a trade.	9. _____
The fans will quickly _ the difference between the two teams.	10. _____
When the students started the day with Mass, they could _ their lessons.	11. _____
Mother Marie will_ a special novena prayer after each Station.	12. _____
Dr. Mike was able to _ his first aid skills when I tripped on the rocks.	13. _____
Aunt Betty had _ bruises on her leg after she fell.	14. _____
"If that clock is _, we need to leave for confession now!"	15. _____

CROSSWORD PUZZLE Use the words from this lesson to complete the crossword puzzle.

ACROSS

2   correct; true

3   to tell the difference

9   certain way of doing something

10 to be slow or doubtful in acting or
    deciding; to pause out of uncertainty

11 to become expert at something

DOWN

1   several

4   to put in; to add to

5   unknown; not recognizable

6   to identify or to decide as the result of
    study or investigation

7   to relate; to have to do with

8   sureness; trust

LESSON 2

MATT AND THE LARGE OX

Matt is taking a snooze on the porch. Aunt Nell startles him when he hears her call out, "Matt, please fetch the large ox from the barn for me."

Still foggy with sleep, Matt asks, "Why?"

"Because I need it now," she demands. "Go!"

Matt makes a feeble attempt to protest but, as always, Aunt Nell remains firm.

Meekly, Matt heads for the barn. He braces himself and goes in. With supreme effort, he ties a rope around the ox's neck. He pulls and he pushes; the ox pushes and pulls. Both pant all the way back to the house.

Aunt Nell giggles from the porch, "Oh, Matt! I did not mean to mislead you. I asked you to fetch the large box, not the large ox!"

A sheepish look comes over Matt's face. He shakes his head and turns to return the ox to the barn. "I need a nap," he mumbles.

EXERCISE A In the reading above, underline the words (or form of the words) that appear in the list below. Write the dictionary definition for the specific part of speech (noun, verb, adjective, or adverb) as used in the reading.

1. snooze (n.) _____

2. startle (v.) _____

3. fetch (v.) _____

4. demand (v.) _____

5. feeble (adj.) _____

6. protest (v.) _____

7. firm (adj.) _____

8. meekly (adv.) _____

9. brace (v.) _____

10. supreme (adj.) _____

11. pant (v.) _____

12. giggle (v.) _____

13. mislead (v.) _____

14. sheepish (adj.) _____

15. mumble (v.) _____

EXERCISE B Circle the correct word.

1. Which word relates to something that is unexpected?

    a) **mumble**   b) **demand**   c) **startle**   d) **giggle**

2. Which word relates to embarrassment?

    a) **fetch**   b) **brace**   c) **supreme**   d) **sheepish**

3. Which word may result in a mistake?

    a) **feeble**   b) **mislead**   c) **protest**   d) **meekly**

4. Which word describes a *strong* statement?

    a) **firm**   b) **feeble**   c) **sheepish**   d) **meekly**

5. Which word does NOT involve one's voice?

    a) **giggle**   b) **fetch**   c) **mumble**   d) **protest**

EXERCISE C Circle two words which either are similar or opposite meanings. Write the letter **S** if they are similar, or **O** if they are opposite. *Optional:* Use a thesaurus for more synonyms and antonyms for Exercise A words.

1. snooze   feeble   startle   nap   _____

2. fetch   mislead   return   stretch   _____

3. feeble   pant   weak   brace   _____

4. object (v.)   protest   effort   ox   _____

5. mumble   shout   brace   mislead   _____

EXERCISE D

Write on the line the correct list word to complete each sentence.

The family prayed the rosary to _ themselves for the coming storm.	1.
Jesus' Crucifixion was the _ sacrifice.	2.
St. Bernadette felt _ because she forgot the catechism answer.	3.
Martha took a quick _ after working long hours at St. Luke's hospital.	4.
Mom said we should speak clearly and not _ as we say our Act of Contrition.	5.
Our dog Rusty likes to _ the newspaper.	6.
The child began to _ with joy after the miraculous cure by St. Francis.	7.
The young priest was _ in his commitment to serve the poor.	8.
The phone's ring did _ me from my nap!	9.
We are all called to _ any evils we see around us.	10.
The old man made a _ cry for help.	11.
When St. Francis appeared, the wild dog sat and began to _ quietly.	12.
Older children should be careful not to _ younger children by bad example.	13.
Jesus does not _ but asks that we love Him.	14.
Animals would kneel _ in front of St. Francis when he called them.	15.

CROSSWORD PUZZLE Use the words from this lesson to complete the crossword puzzle.

ACROSS

5 to argue or object; to speak against or complain

7 to laugh with high-pitched, silly, or nervous sounds

9 weak

11 to speak in an unclear way or too softly to be understood

13 submissively; without argument

14 to take quick breaths

DOWN

1 utmost; extreme

2 short nap

3 embarrassed

4 to cause to jump suddenly in alarm

6 solid; difficult to move

8 to insist or command

9 to go after something

10 to make ready to stand against pressure or attack

12 to guide in a wrong direction; to lead to misunderstanding

LESSON 3

PARTS OF A BOOK

Books may look different in some ways, but they all have similarities. To start, they all have a front cover and a back cover. The covers are joined by a spine, the "backbone" of a book. The name of a book is called its title. The writer is known as its author. Both the title and the author's name appear on the spine and the front cover of the book. They are found also on the title page inside the front cover. A table of contents in the front helps us to identify the material the book addresses. The table of contents tells us the pages or the sections of the book where we can locate the information. Sometimes the table of contents lists each chapter in the book. In some books, there is an index at the back of the book. The index lists words in alphabetical order to assist us to look up information that is inside the book. Look for these items the next time you pick up a book.

EXERCISE A In the reading above, underline the words (or form of the words) that appear in the list below. Write the dictionary definition for the specific part of speech (noun, verb, adjective, or adverb) as used in the reading.

1. similarity (n.) _____

2. spine (n.) _____

3. title (n.) _____

4. author (n.) _____

5. appear (v.) _____

6. table (n.) _____

7. contents (n.) _____

8. identify (v.) _____

9. address (v.) _____

10. section (n.) _____

11. locate (v.) _____

12. chapter (n.) _____

13. index (n.) _____

14. alphabetical (adj.) _____

15. assist (v.) _____

EXERCISE B Circle the correct word.

1. Which word is NOT part of a book?

   a) title   b) chapter   c) index   d) locate

2. Which part of a book is its "backbone"?

   a) contents   b) spine   c) similarity   d) index

3. Which word means a *list*?

   a) table   b) title   c) author   d) section

4. Which word means *help*?

   a) appear   b) locate   c) read   d) assist

5. Which word means *writer*?

   a) author   b) title   c) contents   d) index

EXERCISE C Circle two words which either are similar or opposite meanings. Write the letter **S** if they are similar, or **O** if they are opposite. *Optional:* Use a thesaurus for more synonyms and antonyms for Exercise A words.

1. assist   spine   prevent   publication   _____

2. likeness   similarity   title   index   _____

3. appear   locate   lose   identify   _____

4. author   writer   contents   address   _____

5. index   similarity   author   list   _____

EXERCISE D   Write on the line the correct list word to complete each sentence.

The _ of contents listed all the New Testament books of the Bible.	1.
The librarian offered to _ the boys to find the book, *St. Anne*.	2.
The Picture Bible includes an _ at the back to find the Bible stories.	3.
In 1917, at Fatima, thousands of people waited for Our Lady to _.	4.
Sister Margaret asked us to list the apostles in _ order.	5.
"Can you _ which of the apostles wrote the four Gospels?"	6.
My mother has read her Bible so many times, the _ has fallen off!	7.
"Can you _ the story in the Bible about Daniel in the lions' den?"	8.
The story of Adam and Eve is in the first _ of the Book of Genesis.	9.
The last _ of our Bible is an index of maps.	10.
There is a great deal of _ between the two paintings of Jesus.	11.
"What is the _ of that book about Mother Teresa?"	12.
"Who is the _ of that book about St. Paul?"	13.
In his talk, Father Brown will _ the topic of charity.	14.
The _ of the four Gospels are about the life and teachings of Jesus.	15.

CROSSWORD PUZZLE   Use the words from this lesson to complete the crossword puzzle.

ACROSS

1 to help; to aid

4 backbone

6 main division of a book or story

8 to speak or write about particular topics

12 to look for and find something

14 list

15 subjects or topics treated (as in a book)

DOWN

2 a part of a written book

3 to point out a specific person or thing

5 a list of items in a book and where they may be found

7 in the order of letters of the alphabet

9 resemblance; likeness

10 person who writes something such as a book

11 name of something such as a book or play

13 to show up; to come into view

LESSON 4

AUNT SARAH'S DUCK

"Let's go and find the duck!" Timmy said excitedly.

"What duck?" Lucy asked.

Timmy just yanked her by the arm to the back porch. Before them, a colorful spider web that sparkled with morning dew was clinging to the porch railing and the house. The spider had woven delicate filaments into a beautiful design. Though fragile, the web could endure through wind and rain.

Lucy said in awe, "It is spectacular!"

"Oh, never mind that. Let's find the duck!" Timmy insisted.

"What duck?" Lucy asked again.

Timmy ignored her as he tried to squat under the web. Just then, Aunt Sarah called out, "What are you children looking for?"

"The duck you said is under the spider web," Timmy said.

"Duck? Oh, Timmy, you are mistaken," Aunt Sarah chuckled. "What I said was, 'Duck under the spider web!' The web is so beautiful, I did not want you to walk into it and disturb it!"

Timmy blushed as Lucy and his aunt laughed.

EXERCISE A   In the reading above, underline the words (or form of the words) that appear in the list below. Write the dictionary definition for the specific part of speech (noun, verb, adjective, or adverb) as used in the reading.

1. yank (v.) _____

2. dew (n.) _____

3. cling (v.) _____

4. delicate (adj.) _____

5. filament (n.) _____

6. design (n.) _____

7. fragile (adj.) _____

8. endure (v.) _____

9. awe (n.) _____

10. spectacular (adj.) _____

11. insist (v.) _____

12. squat (v.) _____

13. mistaken (adj.) _____

14. chuckle (v.) _____

15. blush (v.) _____

EXERCISE B Circle the correct word.

1. Which word tells how one might pull a loose tooth?

   a) endure   b) insist   c) yank   d) squat

2. Which word might describe a butterfly's wings?

   a) mistaken   b) delicate   c) dew   d) chuckle

3. Which word describes a gorgeous sunset?

   a) spectacular   b) fragile   c) cling   d) blush

4. Which word describes what we do when we hear a joke?

   a) yank   b) insist   c) design   d) chuckle

5. What do we find on cool grass early in the morning?

   a) awe   b) dew   c) design   d) cling

EXERCISE C Circle two words which either are similar or opposite meanings. Write the letter **S** if they are similar, or **O** if they are opposite. *Optional:* Use a thesaurus for more synonyms and antonyms for Exercise A words.

1. fragile   mistaken   spectacular   delicate   _____

2. endure   chuckle   stop   blush   _____

3. awe   wonder   filament   design   _____

4. squat   cling   blush   yank   _____

5. cling   mistaken   correct   blush   _____

EXERCISE D

Write on the line the correct list word to complete each sentence.

"That antique lace wedding gown of grandmother's is very _!"	1. _____
We _ whenever we hear Father Collins tell that funny story!	2. _____
"Wow! I am in _ of how well Mark sang at the Christmas Mass!"	3. _____
A golden _ was woven into the altar cloth.	4. _____
Because the St. Joseph statue was _, Mom carried it very carefully.	5. _____
Catholics everywhere began to _ that Padre Pio be made a saint.	6. _____
Sally began to _ when the guests praised her beautiful prayer.	7. _____
"Be careful not to pull or _ the crown off the statue of Mary!"	8. _____
The appearance of the sun at Fatima was so _, people fell to their knees.	9. _____
Gideon asked God for a miracle by putting _ on his fleece of wool.	10. _____
You must _ down to see into the prison where St. Peter was chained.	11. _____
The unique _ of each snowflake is enough to prove the existence of God.	12. _____
The children would _ to the cloak of Jesus as He walked the streets.	13. _____
The Magi knew they were not _ by following the star to the King of kings.	14. _____
St. Francis Xavier had to _ many hardships to convert the pagans.	15. _____

CROSSWORD PUZZLE

Use the words from this lesson to complete the crossword puzzle.

ACROSS

2 to demand

7 to last

8 to jerk; to pull strongly

9 to duck; to lower oneself by bending the knees completely

10 easily breakable

11 pattern

12 to become red in the face from embarrassment

14 fine; dainty

DOWN

1 incorrect

3 unusually beautifully; awesome

4 to laugh quietly

5 feeling of wonder

6 thin thread

13 to hold fast by grasping

14 drops of moisture that form on cool surfaces during the night

LESSON
5

O U G H - O U C H !

Ben, a rather smug young man, thought he knew how to get through tough *ough* words.
After all, he had fought a crowd and bought the book he had sought. On his way home, he stopped
under a bough and began to cough. A chill thoroughly pierced him. That was rough. He knew he
ought to hurry home. Ben was not alone, though. He felt a frown furrow his forehead as he watched
a stubborn sow plod through slough to its trough. It was fortunate there had been no drought
the previous spring! At home, Ben's mom was busy with bread dough. We could go on with *ough*
words, I suppose, but this is truly quite enough!

EXERCISE A In the reading above, underline the words (or form of the words) that appear in the list below. Write the dictionary definition for the specific part of speech (noun, verb, adjective, or adverb) as used in the reading.

1. rather (adv.) _____

2. smug (adj.) _____

3. bough (n.) _____

4. thoroughly (adv.) _____

5. frown (n.) _____

6. furrow (v.) _____

7. stubborn (adj.) _____

8. sow (n.) _____

9. plod (v.) _____

10. slough (n.) _____

11. trough (n.) _____

12. fortunate (adj.) _____

13. drought (n.) _____

14. previous (adj.) _____

15. dough (n.) _____

EXERCISE B Circle the correct word.

1. Which word describes someone who is NOT humble?

   a) previous   b) smug   c) stubborn   d) slough

2. Which word means to clean a room *through and through*?

   a) rather   b) fortunately   c) thoroughly   d) previous

3. What might a confused person wear on his face?

   a) frown   b) plod   c) trough   d) dough

4. What might result if there is too little rain?

   a) furrow   b) dough   c) bough   d) drought

5. How might we move in mud that is up to our knees?

   a) plod   b) slough   c) thoroughly   d) fortunately

EXERCISE C Circle two words which either are similar or opposite meanings. Write the letter **S** if they are similar, or **O** if they are opposite. *Optional:* Use a thesaurus for more synonyms and antonyms for Exercise A words.

1. smug   rather   sow   somewhat   _____

2. branch   dough   trough   bough   _____

3. unlucky   fortunate   stubborn   thoroughly   _____

4. drought   dough   previous   preceding   _____

5. sow   rooster   bull   pig   _____

EXERCISE D Write on the line the correct list word to complete each sentence.

"Jimmy, don't make a _ when you are asked to help your dad!"	1. _____
Weak and blind, Samson was forced to _ in a circle around a grindstone.	2. _____
The three-year famine and _ were a hardship for the village people.	3. _____
Uncle Joe was _ surprised by the award from the bishop.	4. _____
The _ had a litter of nine piglets.	5. _____
The animals rejected the food in the _ and knelt in front of the Baby Jesus.	6. _____
To have food for the long journey with Moses, the Jewish people wrapped _ in their cloaks.	7. _____
We saw a frown _ Dad's forehead as he tried to repair the window.	8. _____
The _ Pharisee looked down on the humble Publican.	9. _____
As the soldiers trod through the _, the chaplain prayed for help.	10. _____
The gardener picked up the _ which fell from the ancient tree in the Garden of Gethsemane.	11. _____
We are _ to have three priests available to say Mass.	12. _____
The pastor told the children not to be _ but to be obedient to their parents.	13. _____
On the _ evening, the church choir sang Christmas carols.	14. _____
The Williams family _ cleaned the church before Christmas Mass.	15. _____

CROSSWORD PUZZLE   Use the words from this lesson to complete the crossword puzzle.

ACROSS

2 receiving some unexpected good; lucky

5 a time of little or no rain

6 wet flour used for pastries and bread

8 a wet muddy place

9 not willing to give up

10 preceding; coming before

12 to move forward in a slow but steady manner

13 wrinkling of the brow (the part of the forehead between the eyes)

14 a long open container that holds food for farm animals

DOWN

1 a large branch of a tree

3 somewhat

4 completely

7 to make a groove or wrinkle

8 female pig

11 quite satisfied with oneself

LESSON
6

CONNECTIONS

We do not realize how much we depend on others to survive. We need farmers to grow food

and to bring their harvest to market. The farmers who raise cattle furnish us with food, milk, and

hides. People turn hides into leather which is used for clothes and shoes. Truck drivers transport

these products to our towns. Then we buy what we need from merchants. Thanks to architects and

workers in construction, we have homes in which to live. We all have talents. If we cooperate, we

can live together in harmony.

EXERCISE A In the reading above, underline the words (or form of the words) that appear in the list below. Write the dictionary definition for the specific part of speech (noun, verb, adjective, or adverb) as used in the reading.

1. realize (v.) _____

2. depend (v.) _____

3. survive (v.) _____

4. harvest (n.) _____

5. cattle (n.) _____

6. furnish (v.) _____

7. hide (n.) _____

8. transport (v.) _____

9. product (n.) _____

10. merchant (n.) _____

11. architect (n.) _____

12. construction (n.) _____

13. talent (n.) _____

14. cooperate (v.) _____

15. harmony (n.) _____

EXERCISE B Circle the correct word.

1. What word suggests we all *do our part as a team*?

    a) survive   b) furnish   c) transport   d) cooperate

2. What is the result when people get along together?

    a) harvest   b) harmony   c) hide   d) talent

3. From which person do we buy what we need?

    a) merchant   b) architect   c) construction   d) product

4. Which activity takes place at the end of the growing season?

    a) realize   b) depend   c) harvest   d) cooperate

5. Which word suggest that parents *give us what we need*?

    a) depend   b) furnish   c) talent   d) transport

EXERCISE C Circle two words which either are similar or opposite meanings. Write the letter **S** if they are similar, or **O** if they are opposite. *Optional:* Use a thesaurus for more synonyms and antonyms for Exercise A words.

1. realize   understand   depend   cooperate   _____

2. rely   survive   drill   depend   _____

3. harvest   transport   merchant   carry   _____

4. talent   architect   harmony   skill   _____

5. depend   live   survive   cattle   _____

EXERCISE D

Write on the line the correct list word to complete each sentence.

Ken used his singing _, a great gift from God, to sing in the church choir.	1. _____
The breath of the _ in the stable kept the Holy Family warm.	2. _____
The father of St. Francis was a wealthy _ who could not understand his son.	3. _____
Mom and Dad said the children should _ in cleaning the house on Saturday.	4. _____
The imprisoned man could _ because of his faith.	5. _____
We _ we have a duty to care for those who are hungry or in need.	6. _____
The tepee was covered with a buffalo _.	7. _____
Joseph told Pharoah to store the _ of grain.	8. _____
God gave Solomon wisdom as he became the _ and builder of the Great Temple.	9. _____
If we work together in _ , we can finish the project quickly.	10. _____
The congregation agreed to _ food and money for the African missionaries.	11. _____
Catholic Charities will _ the food and clothes to the missionary hospital.	12. _____
The monks will be responsible for the _ of the new monastery.	13. _____
To support the convent, the chief _ made by the nuns is fruit cakes.	14. _____
The holy souls in Purgatory _ on our prayers.	15. _____

CROSSWORD PUZZLE   Use the words from this lesson to complete the crossword puzzle.

ACROSS

1   natural gift, skill, or ability

8   to be aware of or to understand something

9   agreement

11 the skin of an animal

12 something that is built or put together

13 to work together

14 farm animals such as cows and bulls

DOWN

1   to carry from place to place

2   to supply what is needed

3   to rely

4   to be able to live

5   person who designs buildings

6   person who sells items

7   something that results from labor

10 a ripe crop

LESSON 7

A TURNING POINT

Sonny gaped in disbelief as the older boy snatched a pack of trading cards, tucked them in his pocket, and then sauntered out of the store. Sonny was a witness to a shoplifter in action! It had seemed so easy. A thought flickered in Sonny's mind: "Maybe I can do that, too!"

Sonny glanced around the store, hardly daring to move. The clerk was occupied with a patron. Cautiously, he approached the display of trading cards.

Suddenly, a voice jolted Sonny to attention: "Don't do it, Sonny. It's wrong!" It was the voice of Sonny's conscience. Feeling tremendous relief, Sonny chose a pack of trading cards, paid for them at the counter, and left the store whistling.

EXERCISE A In the reading above, underline the words (or form of the words) that appear in the list below. Write the dictionary definition for the specific part of speech (noun, verb, adjective, or adverb) as used in the reading.

1. gape (v.) _____

2. disbelief (n.) _____

3. snatch (v.) _____

4. tuck (v.) _____

5. saunter (v.) _____

6. witness (n.) _____

7. shoplifter (n.) _____

8. flicker (v.) _____

9. glance (v.) _____

10. hardly (adv.) _____

11. occupy (v.) _____

12. patron (n.) _____

13. cautiously (adv.) _____

14. jolt (v.) _____

15. tremendous (adj.) _____

EXERCISE B

Circle the correct word.

1. Which word relates to a look on someone's face?

    a) gape   b) saunter   c) shoplifter   d) cautiously

2. Which action word is always done quickly?

    a) gape   b) saunter   c) snatch   d) witness

3. Which word is important to a store?

    a) flicker   b) occupy   c) disbelief   d) patron

4. Which word suggests a sudden movement?

    a) patron   b) jolt   c) saunter   d) gape

5. Which word may describe something major?

    a) tuck   b) tremendous   c) occupied   d) jolt

EXERCISE C

Circle two words which either are similar or opposite meanings. Write the letter **S** if they are similar, or **O** if they are opposite. *Optional:* Use a thesaurus for more synonyms and antonyms for Exercise A words.

1. run   snatch   tuck   saunter   _____

2. patron   customer   disbelief   harvest   _____

3. gape   jolt   glance   occupy   _____

4. flicker   witness   tuck   person   _____

5. hardly   disbelief   barely   cautiously   _____

EXERCISE D Write on the line the correct list word to complete each sentence.

The priest heard the confession of the _ at the jail.	1.
The guests began to_ at the woman as she washed the feet of Jesus.	2. _____
Mom and Dad like to _ the children in bed before they fall asleep.	3. _____
The Chosen People _ carried the Ark of the Covenant given to Moses.	4. _____
The sunny June day was perfect for people to _ in the park.	5. _____
My uncle was a _ of the auto accident.	6. _____
No sounds in the church could _ Saint Pio from his ecstasy during the Mass.	7. _____
The news caused a frown to _ on his forehead.	8. _____
Laura stared in _ as the altar boys responded in perfect Latin at the Easter Mass.	9. _____
St. Joseph of Cupertino was not able to _ the statue before it fell to the ground!	10. _____
The honest _ returned the extra book to the store.	11. _____
Father Vincent will _ his afternoon by visiting the children in the hospital.	12. _____
The congregation gave a _ gift to the parish, a painting of St. Joseph.	13. _____
Grandma could _ speak because she was so surprised by our visit.	14. _____
The policeman quickly turned to _ in the direction of the loud noise.	15. _____

CROSSWORD PUZZLE

Use the words from this lesson to complete the crossword puzzle.

ACROSS

2 to walk in a slow and relaxed way

8 great; amazing

9 to flash up and die away quickly

10 to take hold of something quickly or suddenly

12 a person who steals merchandise secretly from a store

15 carefully

DOWN

1 customer

3 difficulty to accept the truth of something

4 to stare with open mouth

5 to look quickly

6 a person who sees an action

7 to move or cause to move in a sudden or jerking way

11 barely

13 to be busy with someone or something

14 to put in a snug or safe place

LESSON
8

THE SEED PROJECT

Clara and Helen shivered slightly. They could hardly conceal their excitement. They had implored their mom to let them plant sunflower seeds, and she had agreed to let them. Helen shook the bag of soil vigorously to break up any clumps. Then both the girls filled the ten flower pots to the brim with soil. Gently, Clara pressed one seed into each pot with her thumb. Helen watered them all. Then they waited.

One week later, they gasped in amazement. They could detect bits of green sprouts beginning to emerge from the soil! Soon the sprouts would become seedlings. Once they were planted outdoors, tall yellow flowers eventually would sway in the breeze. The girls were very pleased that their project had been so successful.

EXERCISE A In the reading above, underline the words (or form of the words) that appear in the list below. Write the dictionary definition for the specific part of speech (noun, verb, adjective, or adverb) as used in the reading.

1. shiver (v.) _____

2. slightly (adv.) _____

3. conceal (v.) _____

4. implore (v.) _____

5. vigorously (adv.) _____

6. clump (n.) _____

7. brim (n.) _____

8. gasp (v.) _____

9. amazement (n.) _____

10. detect (v.) _____

11. sprout (n.) _____

12. emerge (v.) _____

13. seedling (n.) _____

14. eventually (adv.) _____

15. sway (v.) _____

EXERCISE B   Circle the correct word.

1. Which word means to *ask* or *beg*?

   a) emerge   b) implore   c) detect   d) sway

2. How might we react when the temperature is 35 degrees?

   a) conceal   b) implore   c) shiver   d) sway

3. What do we do when we *tuck* something under a pile?

   a) clump   b) brim   c) conceal   d) gasp

4. Which word describes something that moves *only a little bit*?

   a) slightly   b) eventually   c) vigorously   d) shiver

5. Which word relates to something that takes our breath away?

   a) seedling   b) sprout   c) clump   d) amazement

EXERCISE C   Circle two words which either are similar or opposite meanings. Write the letter **S** if they are similar, or **O** if they are opposite. ***Optional:*** Use a thesaurus for more synonyms and antonyms for Exercise A words.

1. vigorously   slowly   implore   gasp   _____

2. hide   implore   emerge   sway   _____

3. soil   sway   sprout   swing   _____

4. brim   clump   middle   edge   _____

5. gasp   glance   breathe in   grin   _____

EXERCISE D   Write on the line the correct list word to complete each sentence.

The wide _ of the missionary's hat protected him from the hot sun!	1. _____
We began to _ as we walked through the cold wind to Christmas Mass.	2. _____
Jesus taught that even the smallest _ can produce a great tree.	3. _____
The apostles stared in _ as the huge crowd gathered to hear Jesus speak.	4. _____
We need to _ defend ourselves against the dangers of bad companions.	5. _____
It is amazing that with a small _ of soil, God can make a seed produce a flower.	6. _____
When Jesus called his name, they were amazed to see Lazarus _ from the tomb!	7. _____
The people _ aloud when they see Lazarus walk out of the tomb!	8. _____
After Jesus cured the crippled boy, no one could _ even a limp!	9. _____
He will need to study more, but _ Joey will know the facts.	10. _____
As the enemies' wheat began to _ in the wind, Samson set it on fire!	11. _____
With God on his side, David was not even _ afraid of Goliath!	12. _____
Little David had to _ King Saul to let him fight Goliath!	13. _____
David did not _ that his only weapon was a slingshot!	14. _____
The little green _ will grow into a large corn stalk.	15. _____

CROSSWORD
PUZZLE   Use the words from this lesson to complete the crossword puzzle.

ACROSS

1   to humbly make a request

3   edge; rim

6   to shake from cold or fear

11 a young plant growing from a seed

12 to hide

13 young stem of a plant that is growing from a seed

15 sooner or later; in due time

DOWN

2   to come forth

4   to a small degree

5   to suddenly take in a breath

7   with strength; with energy

8   to discover or notice the presence of something

9   great surprise

10 something that is packed or clustered together

14 to swing slowly from side to side

LESSON 9

MOVING ALONG

It would be boring to simply walk all the time, or sit, or stand. It is much more fun to meander through a park, stride into the kitchen, or whip through a supermarket. Children do not just stand up. They leap from their chairs, or they tumble out of them! Kittens strut across a lawn, squirrels scamper, and snakes slither. Tall men unfold out of a car, dogs bolt from a car, and teenagers slump in the back seat. Brides glide down the aisle, and skaters whirl around an ice rink. Trees shudder in the nippy autumn breeze. Leaves waltz to the ground. Movement adds excitement to our lives!

EXERCISE A In the reading above, underline the words (or form of the words) that appear in the list below. Write the dictionary definition for the specific part of speech (noun, verb, adjective, or adverb) as used in the reading.

1. meander (v.) _____

2. stride (v.) _____

3. whip (v.) _____

4. leap (v.) _____

5. tumble (v.) _____

6. strut (v.) _____

7. scamper (v.) _____

8. slither (v.) _____

9. bolt (v.) _____

10. slump (v.) _____

11. glide (v.) _____

12. whirl (v.) _____

13. shudder (v.) _____

14. nippy (adj.) _____

15. waltz (v.) _____

EXERCISE B

Circle the correct word.

1. Which word does NOT belong in this group?

   a) whip   b) leap   c) bolt   d) slump

2. Which word does NOT describe the way a rabbit moves?

   a) slither   b) tumble   c) scamper   d) bolt

3. Which word does NOT describe movement along a straight line?

   a) stride   b) meander   c) strut   d) bolt

4. Which word does NOT relate to slow movement?

   a) slither   b) glide   c) waltz   d) leap

5. Which word does NOT describe the way a self-confident person walks?

   a) stride   b) strut   c) slump   d) glide

EXERCISE C

Circle two words which either are similar or opposite meanings. Write the letter **S** if they are similar, or **O** if they are opposite. *Optional:* Use a thesaurus for more synonyms and antonyms for Exercise A words.

1. glide   shudder   waltz   nippy   _____

2. meander   leap   jump   waltz   _____

3. bolt   shudder   nippy   meander   _____

4. whirl   nippy   strut   slump   _____

5. run   slither   tumble   scamper   _____

EXERCISE D   Write on the line the correct list word to complete each sentence.

There was a chill in the air, a _ breeze blowing from the ocean!	1. _____
The elderly man with a cane began to _ into his pew.	2. _____
The puppies _ up to their bowl at feeding time.	3. _____
The brothers liked to _ around the floor with their dad!	4. _____
Peter's reaction was to _ from the boat and walk on the water toward Jesus.	5. _____
When Moses lifted up his hand, the waters of the Red Sea began to _ around the Egyptian soldiers.	6. _____
On their anniversary, Grandpa asked Grandma to _ to the music!	7. _____
My brother likes to _ down the hallway taking steps that are three feet long!	8. _____
"Don't _, Stephen, on your way back, or you will be late for dinner!"	9. _____
For the competition, Kathy taught her horse how to _ and trot.	10. _____
Whenever Danny approaches, the deer suddenly _ for the woods!	11. _____
Shaped like a snake, the devil began to _ down the tree to tempt Eve!	12. _____
The small plane carrying the missionary seemed to _ onto the ground.	13. _____
As the wind began to _ through the old church, the candles blew out.	14. _____
St. Roch did not _ or hesitate to help the sick during the Great Plague.	15. _____

CROSSWORD PUZZLE Use the words from this lesson to complete the crossword puzzle.

ACROSS

2 to move forward suddenly and quickly

4 to tremble; to shiver

7 to move quickly, sometimes in a jerking way

8 to jump from a surface

9 to walk in long steps

10 to turn or move in circles quickly

11 to move in a smooth, even, quiet motion

12 chilly

DOWN

1 to walk stiffly and in a proud manner

3 to move along a winding (curving) course

4 to move in a sliding motion like a snake

5 to roll and turn

6 to run lightly but in a quick and hurried manner.

9 to slide down; to slouch

10 to dance or move in a graceful, gliding manner

LESSON 10

THE PORPOISE WITH A PURPOSE

A porpoise named Dorcas is the star performer at the children's aquarium. She sweeps gracefully through the water. Then she leaps up high, turns a somersault, and swoops down again causing a gigantic splash. The children roar with gleeful applause. The young ones stare eagerly over the water. Suddenly, Dorcas darts into the air once more. With thrill and excitement, the little ones jump from their seats with screams of laughter. Dorcas seems completely happy. She never seems to feel boredom or fatigue. Why does she love to perform? Is it for glory? Is it for fame? Mother explains, "The reason Dorcas performs is because God wants to hear the sweet laughter of children as they enjoy His beautiful creatures."

EXERCISE A In the reading above, underline the words (or form of the words) that appear in the list below. Write the dictionary definition for the specific part of speech (noun, verb, adjective, or adverb) as used in the reading.

1. performer (n.) _____
2. aquarium (n.) _____
3. sweep (v.) _____
4. gracefully (adv.) _____
5. swoop (v.) _____
6. gigantic (adj.) _____
7. gleeful (adj.) _____
8. applause (n.) _____
9. stare (v.) _____
10. dart (v.) _____
11. thrill (n.) _____
12. boredom (n.) _____
13. fatigue (n.) _____
14. glory (n.) _____
15. fame (n.) _____

EXERCISE B   Circle the correct word.

1. Which word means someone who uses skills in front of an audience?

    a)   **applause**   b)   **fatigue**   c)   **fame**   d)   **performer**

2. Which word describes children squealing joyfully?

    a)   **gracefully**   b)   **gleeful**   c)   **gigantic**   d)   **glory**

3. Which word relates to the wind brushing leaves off a lawn?

    a)   **stare**   b)   **dart**   c)   **sweep**   d)   **boredom**

4. Which word relates to looking at something in awe?

    a)   **stare**   b)   **aquarium**   c)   **gigantic**   d)   **boredom**

5. Which word describes the excitement by all A's on a report card?

    a)   **thrill**   b)   **fame**   c)   **stare**   d)   **swoop**

EXERCISE C   Circle two words which either are similar or opposite meanings. Write the letter **S** if they are similar, or **O** if they are opposite. *Optional:* Use a thesaurus for more synonyms and antonyms for Exercise A words.

1. fame   glory   swoop   performer   _____

2. hardly   gracefully   happily   smoothly   _____

3. boredom   sweep   stare   thrill   _____

4. large   gleeful   gigantic   dart   _____

5. fatigue   energy   applause   porpoise   _____

EXERCISE D Write on the line the correct list word to complete each sentence.

Daddy bought an _ for Susie's fish.	1. _____
Though Susie was sick, she enjoyed watching one playful fish who was quite a _.	2. _____
Susie's enthusiastic _ showed her approval and joy for his performance!	3. _____
Daddy knew there would be no _ for Susie as she watched her fish.	4. _____
The orange and red fish would _ this way and that way.	5. _____
A larger fish swam slowly and _ around the small playful fish.	6. _____
As Billy entered the room, the larger fish made a _ splash.	7. _____
As Billy's hand and arm _ across the table, the aquarium falls to the floor.	8. _____
The cat ran to _ down on the fish and to play with them.	9. _____
Susie could only _ at the cat and the fish; then she screamed.	10. _____
It was no _ for Mom as she ran into the room!	11. _____
Daddy gained new _ in Susie's eyes when he picked up the fish!	12. _____
The cat was not as _ after Daddy took away her fish toys!	13. _____
Susie seemed to feel _ after this emotional adventure and took a nap!	14. _____
"Let's give _ to God for the entertainment His creatures provide!"	15. _____

Use the words from this lesson to complete the crossword puzzle.

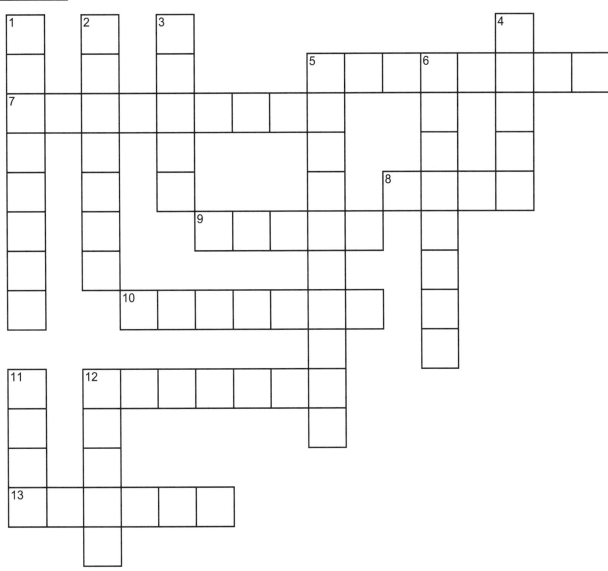

ACROSS

5   huge; very large

7   someone who does something that needs skill

8   a condition in which one is well-known and well-liked

9   to move swiftly through water or over a surface

10   feeling of being very tired in mind or body

12   full of delight; joyous

13   a sudden feeling of joy

DOWN

1   clapping of the hands to show approval

2   feeling of tiredness because of something dull

3   to rush down onto something

4   to look hard and long at someone or something

5   in an easy or lovely manner

6   building that contains tanks of water with water animals in them

11   to move or jump out suddenly and quickly

12   praise; admiration

LESSON 11

THE ALL DAY TWO-HOUR TRIP

Grand River was the destination for our annual vacation. The whole family packed into the van and we were off. One hour later, Dad said, "Let's be adventurous and take the scenic road. It should be only a half-hour detour."

Everyone groaned except Allen, Dad's ally. "Yes, let's do it!" Allen whooped with enthusiasm, then quickly cried, "Ouch! Don't shove me!"

Mom suggested we stop for directions, but Dad just drove on. Two hours later, Dad pointed and said, "Look at that gorgeous lake!"

"Dad! We passed that lake an hour ago!"

"Are you sure?" he asked.

"We're positive," Mom answered. "We're lost."

Then she said, "I just solved a biblical mystery. The reason it took the Israelites forty years to reach the Promised Land is that after 39 ½ years, Mrs. Moses asked for directions!"

A chorus of laughter rose from the back seats. This time, it was Dad's turn to groan.

EXERCISE A In the reading above, underline the words (or form of the words) that appear in the list below. Write the dictionary definition for the specific part of speech (noun, verb, adjective, or adverb) as used in the reading.

1. destination (n.) _____

2. annual (adj.) _____

3. adventurous (adj.) _____

4. scenic (adj.) _____

5. detour (n.) _____

6. groan (v.) _____

7. ally (n.) _____

8. whoop (v.) _____

9. enthusiasm (n.) _____

10. shove (v.) _____

11. suggest (v.) _____

12. gorgeous (adj.) _____

13. positive (adj.) _____

14. solve (v.) _____

15. chorus (n.) _____

EXERCISE B

Circle the correct word.

1. Which word relates to unhappiness?

    a) whoop   b) suggest   c) groan   d) solve

2. Which word suggests a long way around something?

    a) destination   b) detour   c) ally   d) enthusiasm

3. Which word relates to a reaction to a wonderful surprise?

    a) solve   b) shove   c) groan   d) whoop

4. Which word describes someone who is not afraid to take chances?

    a) adventurous   b) annual   c) scenic   d) gorgeous

5. Which word describes someone who is very sure of an answer?

    a) annual   b) positive   c) adventurous   d) chorus

EXERCISE C

Circle two words which either are similar or opposite meanings. Write the letter **S** if they are similar, or **O** if they are opposite. *Optional:* Use a thesaurus for more synonyms and antonyms for Exercise A words.

1. annual   monthly   weekly   yearly   _____

2. enthusiasm   vacation   excitement   detour   _____

3. ally   enemy   vacation   lake   _____

4. shove   groan   solve   answer   _____

5. boring   gorgeous   positive   ugly   _____

EXERCISE D   Write on the line the correct list word to complete each sentence.

At our _ Easter procession, Father Chris let us have lighted candles.	1.
The _ for the Holy Family was Egypt, to escape the evil King Herod.	2.
Don't _ when your mother asks you to do a chore.	3.
Mom brought home a _ pink hat to wear in the Easter parade.	4.
Uncle Paul had an _ trip on a ship that almost sank!	5.
St. Francis took a _ from his planned route when he met the poor pagans.	6.
Little Dave began to _ with joy when he found his new red tricycle!	7.
Ginny was _ that Mom had baked a special birthday cake for her!	8.
Alex could not _ the math problem his dad had given him.	9.
"Terry, don't _ your little brother! Be kind to him!"	10.
"I would like to _ that we say the Rosary after dinner."	11.
Grandpa was an _ for Tommy in doing his secret science project.	12.
A _ of song filled the chapel on Christmas Eve.	13.
As we sailed along , Dad thanked God for giving us this _ view.	14.
St. Paul showed great _ for teaching about Jesus.	15.

CROSSWORD
PUZZLE   Use the words from this lesson to complete the crossword puzzle.

ACROSS

1   to shout; to cheer

5   providing views of nature's landscape

6   willing to take risks

8   sounds made by a group of persons or animals all at the same time

9   to offer or present an idea

11 to push with force

12 very beautiful

14 place where one plans to go

DOWN

2   completely certain

3   yearly; occurring once a year

4   way around a usual or planned route

6   friend; someone who is on the same side as another

7   strong feeling in support of something

10 to moan

13 to find the answer to something

LESSON 12

HERE COMES TROUBLE

Our dog has managed to find all sorts of mischief since he was a pup. That is how he earned the name Trouble! For instance, after becoming sopping wet in a sudden downpour, Trouble ruined Mom's hallway carpet. Once, when he became bored with his chew-toy, he substituted the leg of the coffee table for his entertainment! Trouble is definitely unpleasant when he drools just before dinner. Trouble was never fond of taking baths, but at every attempt, it is the people who end up drenched and aromatic! After such events, that brown furry dog wriggles out the door and trots away wearing what looks like a grin of victory. He truly is a scamp, but, in spite of all the trouble he causes, we still love Trouble.

EXERCISE A In the reading above, underline the words (or form of the words) that appear in the list below. Write the dictionary definition for the specific part of speech (noun, verb, adjective, or adverb) as used in the reading.

1. manage (v.) _____

2. sort (n.) _____

3. mischief (n.) _____

4. earn (v.) _____

5. sopping (adj.) _____

6. substitute (v.) _____

7. drool (v.) _____

8. fond (adj.) _____

9. attempt (n.) _____

10. drench (v.) _____

11. aromatic (adj.) _____

12. wriggle (v.) _____

13. trot (v.) _____

14. grin (n.) _____

15. scamp (n.) _____

EXERCISE B

Circle the correct word.

1. Which word means *to get something by working for it*?

   a) manage   b) earn   c) substitute   d) trot

2. Which word might describe a bouquet of flowers?

   a) fond   b) drench   c) aromatic   d) sopping

3. Which word relates to using crackers instead of bread?

   a) substitute   b) attempt   c) sort   d) wriggle

4. Which word relates to mothers having affection for their children?

   a) drench   b) aromatic   c) fond   d) grin

5. Which word means *someone who often gets into mischief*?

   a) attempt   b) trouble   c) sort   d) scamp

EXERCISE C

Circle two words which either are similar or opposite meanings. Write the letter **S** if they are similar, or **O** if they are opposite. ***Optional:*** Use a thesaurus for more synonyms and antonyms for Exercise A words.

1. sort   mischief   attempt   trouble   _____

2. substitute   earn   replace   drench   _____

3. sort   fail   manage   mischief   _____

4. trot   substitute   stand   earn   _____

5. attempt   type   sort   wriggle   _____

EXERCISE D

Write on the line the correct list word to complete each sentence.

Jesus cured the crippled man who could not _ to reach the miraculous pool.	1.
The apostles thought the children would cause _ but Jesus said, "Let the children come to Me."	2.
As his horse began to _, St. Paul was thrown off and fell to the ground!	3.
Mom said she had _ memories as a young girl of going to the shrine with grandma.	4.
At Fatima's Miracle of the Sun, thousands of _ wet people were suddenly dry.	5.
The heavy rain threatened to _ the Easter lilies.	6.
That _ of information is available on the Internet.	7.
With a huge _ , Tommy accepted his diploma.	8.
You can _ water for milk in that recipe.	9.
Jenny tried to _ enough money to buy a silver crucifix for Dad.	10.
Those dried rose pedals in the basket are so pretty and _.	11.
Ben, that two-year-old _, ran back and forth during the wedding reception.	12.
Jimmy tried to _ out of his seat, but Dad held him during the Rosary.	13.
The young people made an _ to have a Holy Hour once a week.	14.
My baby brother began to _ while eating his oatmeal.	15.

CROSSWORD PUZZLE

Use the words from this lesson to complete the crossword puzzle.

ACROSS

2 to move away by twisting and turning

7 pleasant smelling

9 to succeed; to find a way to do or get something

10 a wide smile

11 to serve as a replacement

13 like or loving; having affection

14 to let liquid flow out of one's mouth

DOWN

1 to completely wet

3 to get as the result of some effort or action; to deserve

4 kind; type

5 rascal; someone who often gets into mischief

6 thoroughly wet

8 act of trying

9 activity that annoys other

12 to move along quickly

LESSON 13

A SIMPLE WATERMELON SEED

Picture our family enjoying a backyard picnic. Rodney decides to see how far he can shoot a watermelon seed! He blows as hard as he can. The seed is like a missile. It hits the dog on the leg, stings him, and he yelps. The seed bounces off the dog and strikes the baby on the arm. The baby, who is in Mom's arms, suddenly raises his fist in surprise. He knocks Mom's hand which causes her ice cream cone to topple into Dad's lap. Dad jumps up and upsets his lawn chair. The lawn chair was giving some protection to the dog, but now it falls on the dog. Trying to escape, the dog yanks on his leash which is tied to the table umbrella. The umbrella falls over! It is all over in a flash!

Stunned by the events, Rodney says, "That was one powerful watermelon seed!"

EXERCISE A In the reading above, underline the words (or form of the words) that appear in the list below. Write the dictionary definition for the specific part of speech (noun, verb, adjective, or adverb) as used in the reading.

1. picture (v.) _____

2. shoot (v.) _____

3. missile (n.) _____

4. sting (v.) _____

5. yelp (v.) _____

6. strike (v.) _____

7. fist (n.) _____

8. topple (v.) _____

9. lap (n.) _____

10. upset (v.) _____

11. protection (n.) _____

12. yank (v.) _____

13. flash (n.) _____

14. stunned (adj.) _____

15. powerful (adj.) _____

EXERCISE B Circle the correct word.

1. Which word suggests what might happen if books are piled too high?

    a) strike   b) yelp   c) shoot   d) topple

2. A snowball is an example of which word below?

    a) flash   b) missile   c) fist   d) lap

3. Which word may describe winds blowing at 70 miles per hour?

    a) powerful   b) stunned   c) flash   d) protection

4. Which word means *to try to see something without actually looking at it*?

    a) upset   b) yank   c) picture   d) yelp

5. Which word means *to make a quick, high-pitched sound*?

    a) sting   b) topple   c) yank   d) yelp

EXERCISE C Circle two words which either are similar or opposite meanings. Write the letter **S** if they are similar, or **O** if they are opposite. *Optional:* Use a thesaurus for more synonyms and antonyms for Exercise A words.

1. topple   strike   shoot   hit   _____

2. surprised   sting   strike   stunned   _____

3. powerful   protection   flash   hours   _____

4. sting   missile   lap   rocket   _____

5. upset   throw   shoot   picture   _____

EXERCISE D   Write on the line the correct list word to complete each sentence.

"Can you _ us in the beautiful church for our wedding?"	1. _____
When you are riding that horse, do not _ its reins.	2. _____
My baby sister sat on my _ during the Rosary novena.	3. _____
The altar boy was careful not to cause the candles to _ as he lit them.	4. _____
The rocket _ was never launched.	5. _____
The puppy began to _ when its mother left the area.	6. _____
"While you are picking the flowers, don't let those bees _ you!"	7. _____
Do not _ the bag of apples.	8. _____
In a _ , the fireman rescued the man from the fire.	9. _____
Sister Margaret was _ when the children did not know their prayers.	10. _____
The Blessed Mother said at Fatima that the Rosary is a _ prayer.	11. _____
The soldier sewed his St. George medal into his jacket for _ from enemies.	12. _____
The evil man raised his _ before he attempted to arrest the saint.	13. _____
Peter wanted to _ the soldier but then cut off his ear.	14. _____
In archery class, I _ arrows at a target.	15. _____

CROSSWORD PUZZLE   Use the words from this lesson to complete the crossword puzzle.

ACROSS

2   to let fly with force

4   to imagine; to see in one's mind

7   to hit with force

8   very short time

9   to pull suddenly; to jerk

10 object that is shot in order to hit
    something with force

11 the front part of the body from the waist
    to the knees when a person is sitting

12 to cause a painful, burning feeling

DOWN

1   very strong

3   to knock something over

4   safety

5   to fall over; to tumble down

6   hand with fingers bent to form a ball

7   shocked; very surprised

9   to make a quick high-pitched sound

LESSON
14

GUESS WHO?

The family decided to play "Guess Who?" William agreed to go first. He chose to describe Ralph, their rooster.

"He has two rather skinny legs," William began. "His two penetrating eyes seem capable of spotting everything at once."

His family was bewildered, so William continued. "He takes every opportunity to sing. We do not appreciate it when he starts singing at dawn!"

Still, no one guessed. William continued. "He loves to tease. Sometimes when we are outdoors, he chases us!"

Three hands shot up. "I know! I know!" they shouted jointly.

"I know!" piped little Harry. "It's Dad!"

To Harry's great confusion, everyone roared with laughter. William's face turned crimson. Then, when he told Dad it was Ralph the rooster, Dad laughed with them.

EXERCISE A In the reading above, underline the words (or form of the words) that appear in the list below. Write the dictionary definition for the specific part of speech (noun, verb, adjective, or adverb) as used in the reading.

1. agree (v.) _____

2. describe (v.) _____

3. penetrating (adj.) _____

4. seem (v.) _____

5. capable (adj.) _____

6. spot (v.) _____

7. bewilder (v.) _____

8. opportunity (n.) _____

9. appreciate (v.) _____

10. dawn (n.) _____

11. jointly (adv.) _____

12. pipe (v.) _____

13. confusion (n.) _____

14. roar (v.) _____

15. crimson (adj.) _____

EXERCISE B   Circle the correct word.

1.   Which word means *to be thankful* for everything our parents do for us?

a)   agree   b)   appreciate   c)   describe   d)   roar

2.   Which word may describe the sky at sunset?

a)   dawn   b)   bewilder   c)   crimson   d)   capable

3.   Which word means *to see* a friend in a crowd?

a)   describe   b)   penetrating   c)   pipe   d)   spot

4.   Which word may we use to mean water *is soaking through* our clothes?

a)   penetrating   b)   jointly   c)   capable   d)   confusion

5.   Which word might we use when we *tell someone all about* the zoo we visited?

a)   describe   b)   seem   c)   roar   d)   agree

EXERCISE C   Circle two words which either are similar or opposite meanings. Write the letter **S** if they are similar, or **O** if they are opposite. ***Optional:*** Use a thesaurus for more synonyms and antonyms for Exercise A words.

1.   opportunity   spot   sunset   dawn   _____

2.   confusion   understanding   roar   seem   _____

3.   pipe   seem   spot   appear   _____

4.   crimson   penetrating   opportunity   chance   _____

5.   agree   giggle   roar   seem   _____

EXERCISE D   Write on the line the correct list word to complete each sentence.

My brother and I _ own the expensive chess set Daddy found for us.	1.
Mary Magdalen went to the tomb at _ to find Jesus.	2.
We _ the hard work of the missionaries.	3.
Our family had the _ to see the Pope at the Vatican.	4.
"Mom and I _ to take the family to the EWTN Catholic Family Day!"	5.
Father Bernard wore his _ vestments for the Mass for the martyred saint.	6.
The pastor said that Dennis is _ of being an excellent altar boy.	7.
The math problems _ him.	8.
The _ cold made it difficult to be outdoors.	9.
There was _ among the people because they heard that Jesus had risen from the dead.	10.
With great excitement, the small children _ , "Surprise!"	11.
St. Paul said that no one can _ the incredible happiness we will have in heaven.	12.
Mom agreed that her guardian angels _ to help her stay safe.	13.
The pirate was able to _ the treasure in the dimly lit cave.	14.
The happy children will _ with laughter when the clowns appear!	15.

CROSSWORD PUZZLE Use the words from this lesson to complete the crossword puzzle.

ACROSS

3 able; having the ability to do something

6 chance; handy occasion

7 to speak in a high tone of voice

9 to use words to give a picture of someone or something

10 mix-up; lack of understanding

13 piercing; able to go through

15 to fill with doubt; to puzzle; to confuse

DOWN

1 early morning when the sun comes up

2 to see

4 to be grateful

5 dark red

8 to appear

11 together; at the same time

12 to arrive at a common decision

14 to laugh loudly

LESSON 15

SILLY MILLY

Milly had very long arms. She was still growing, and her legs had not yet caught up with the rest of her. Milly was good-natured, though. She laughed with us whenever we affectionately called her "Silly Milly." She even was amused but not embarrassed by some events. Milly could be clumsy and bungle even a simple activity. One time, she had the misfortune of stretching under the ceiling fan. Her hands caught one of the blades. Milly was sent whirling around and around.

Dizzy from the spin, Milly stammered, "M-m-y, m-m-y, m-m-y! That was a rather moving experience, wasn't it?"

In our opinion, what Milly lacked in grace, she made up for in humor.

EXERCISE A In the reading above, underline the words (or form of the words) that appear in the list below. Write the dictionary definition for the specific part of speech (noun, verb, adjective, or adverb) as used in the reading.

1. good-natured (adj.) _____

2. affectionately (adv.) _____

3. amuse (v.) _____

4. embarrass (v.) _____

5. clumsy (adj.) _____

6. bungle (v.) _____

7. misfortune (n.) _____

8. dizzy (adj.) _____

9. stammer (v.) _____

10. moving (adj.) _____

11. experience (n.) _____

12. opinion (n.) _____

13. lack (v.) _____

14. grace (n.) _____

15. humor (n.) _____

EXERCISE B   Circle the correct word.

1. Which word might we use when we burn toast to a crisp?

   a) **bungle**   b) **stammer**   c) **lack**   d) **dizzy**

2. Which word means *to entertain*?

   a) **clumsy**   b) **dizzy**   c) **good-natured**   d) **amuse**

3. Which word might we use when someone *does not speak in a smooth, flowing way*?

   a) **humor**   b) **stammer**   c) **opinion**   d) **affectionately**

4. Which word does NOT apply to a clumsy person?

   a) **grace**   b) **bungle**   c) **misfortune**   d) **embarrass**

5. Which word means *in a kind and loving way*?

   a) **embarrass**   b) **lack**   c) **affectionately**   d) **moving**

EXERCISE C   Circle two words which either are similar or opposite meanings. Write the letter **S** if they are similar, or **0** if they are opposite. *Optional:* Use a thesaurus for more synonyms and antonyms for Exercise A words.

1. dizzy   good-natured   clumsy   angry   _____

2. humor   need   lack   experience   _____

3. good luck   opinion   misfortune   grace   _____

4. clumsy   humor   moving   boring   _____

5. opinion   judgment   experience   misfortune   _____

EXERCISE D

Write on the line the correct list word to complete each sentence.

The O'Brien family had the _ of being snowed in on Sunday.	1.
At the parish dinner, Father Milton gave a _ farewell talk.	2.
Father hired the carpenter so I would not _ the building of the shrine.	3.
I felt _ after dropping the prayer books!	4.
The merry-go-round made me _ .	5.
The new cashier will become faster with more _ .	6.
Grandma _ kissed her newly-baptized grandson.	7.
It is my parents' _ that the family Rosary is an important part of the day.	8.
The jugglers _ the children at our church festival	9.
"Memorize those answers so you don't _ yourself."	10.
The new bride was so overcome she could only _ her "I do."	11.
St. Philip Neri was friendly with everyone; he was very _ .	12.
Because the poor people _ food, our church offers a free soup kitchen.	13.
Having a good sense of _ can help a sick person recover quickly.	14.
My parents waltzed across the dance floor with _ and beauty.	15.

CROSSWORD PUZZLE   Use the words from this lesson to complete the crossword puzzle.

ACROSS

1   bad luck

5   emotional; stirring one's feelings; set into motion

6   ability to see the funny side of a situation

7   lovingly

9   to cause one to be uncomfortable; to upset someone

11 cheerful; rarely angry

12 without ease; not graceful

13 to be without something; to be missing something

14 actual involvement in an activity

DOWN

2   judgment

3   feeling unsteady from spinning

4   to cause something to fail

8   to entertain; to cause to feel happy

10 to speak by repeating or holding sounds

11 ease of motion

LESSON 16

LET THE SHOW BEGIN

The park has few visitors on this drab day. Even so, we sit on a bench, eager to watch the show. The characters soon appear. They are remarkably quick, and they have incredible energy. They do not care one whit for social activities. Anxious about the coming winter, they yearn to gather all the scraps they can. On stubby legs, they scramble left and right, forward and back in a zealous effort to gather seeds and nuts. When they climb the tall trees, these frisky creatures prove to be accomplished acrobats with a keen sense of balance. Squirrels truly can turn a simple visit to the park into an enjoyable experience.

EXERCISE A

In the reading above, underline the words (or form of the words) that appear in the list below. Write the dictionary definition for the specific part of speech (noun, verb, adjective, or adverb) as used in the reading.

1. drab (adj.) _____

2. eager (adj.) _____

3. remarkably (adv.) _____

4. incredible (adj.) _____

5. whit (n.) _____

6. social (adj.) _____

7. anxious (adj.) _____

8. yearn (v.) _____

9. scraps (n.) _____

10. stubby (adj.) _____

11. scramble (v.) _____

12. zealous (adj.) _____

13. frisky (adj.) _____

14. accomplished (adj.) _____

15. keen (adj.) _____

EXERCISE B

Circle the correct word.

1. Which word suggests moving quickly?

    a) yearn   b) scramble   c) stubby   d) anxious

2. Which word suggests a highly unusual manner?

    a) remarkably   b) drab   c) frisky   d) social

3. Which word suggests hard-working?

    a) stubby   b) incredible   c) keen   d) zealous

4. Which word may describe a talented musician?

    a) whit   b) drab   c) accomplished   d) eager

5. Which word may relate to a nervous person?

    a) eager   b) anxious   c) keen   d) social

EXERCISE C

Circle two words which either are similar or opposite meanings. Write the letter **S** if they are similar, or **O** if they are opposite. *Optional:* Use a thesaurus for more synonyms and antonyms for Exercise A words.

1. yearn   scramble   desire   frisky   _____

2. lively   social   frisky   keen   _____

3. stubby   scraps   short   whit   _____

4. eager   impatient   quick   incredible   _____

5. whit   large amount   whip   wish   _____

EXERCISE D

Write on the line the correct list word to complete each sentence.

The _ gathering helped the new pastor meet the parishioners.	1. _____
St. Rita began to _ to enter the convent.	2. _____
Mother did not like the _ color of Mary's dress.	3. _____
The _ little boy could not wait to serve at Mass.	4. _____
St. Francis was a _ saint who was determined to convert the pagans.	5. _____
The children began to _ to find the hidden Easter eggs!	6. _____
Mother had to take the _ baby out of the church hall!	7. _____
He is a _ talented chess player.	8. _____
"Elizabeth is a truly _ violinist!"	9. _____
The dog's _ sense of smell led him to the lost child.	10. _____
Little Bob's _ fingers struggled to find the small beads on the rosary.	11. _____
Sally did not care one _ that she was not chosen to be the May queen.	12. _____
Lazarus was the poor man who ate the _ that fell from the rich man's table.	13. _____
Brother Dominic told us about the _ Miracle of the Sun at Fatima!	14. _____
Jesus said we must not be _ about what we eat or what we wear!	15. _____

CROSSWORD PUZZLE Use the words from this lesson to complete the crossword puzzle.

ACROSS

4 greatly desiring; looking forward to

7 leftover pieces of food; small bits

11 short and thick

13 to move or climb quickly

14 uneasy or nervous about what might happen

15 dull; lacking interest

DOWN

1 very sensitive

2 unusually; in a way that is worthy of notice

3 difficult to believe

5 friendly, interacting with others

6 filled with eagerness

8 skilled; expert

9 a very small amount

10 lively

12 to desire eagerly

LESSON 17

WHAT SHALL WE CALL THE BABY?

The names of the young of some animals are familiar to us. The more common ones are kittens and puppies. We usually refer to most others as "babies." However, various kinds of animal babies have specific names. We should acquaint ourselves with some of these. Some are rather obvious. A baby duck is a duckling, and a baby goose is a gosling. Eagles are call eaglets when they hatch in their nest, called an aerie. Some animal babies have identical names, but they are quite distinct. We know that a cow bears a calf, but so does an elephant and a whale! A hare gives birth to a leveret, horses bear foals, deer have fawns, and goats have kids. It's fun to learn the names of young animals.

EXERCISE A In the reading above, underline the words (or form of the words) that appear in the list below. Write the dictionary definition for the specific part of speech (noun, verb, adjective, or adverb) as used in the reading.

1. young (n.) _____

2. familiar (adj.) _____

3. common (adj.) _____

4. refer (v.) _____

5. various (adj.) _____

6. specific (adj.) _____

7. acquaint (v.) _____

8. obvious (adj.) _____

9. hatch (v.) _____

10. aerie (n.) _____

11. identical (adj.) _____

12. distinct (adj.) _____

13. bear (v.) _____

14. hare (n.) _____

15. foal (n.) _____

EXERCISE B   Circle the correct word.

1. Which word relates to fawns, kittens, and goslings?

    a) **aerie**   b) **hare**   c) **young**   d) **whale**

2. Which word relates to the young of birds?

    a) **acquaint**   b) **hatch**   c) **refer**   d) **obvious**

3. Which word might describe the flavors in a box of mixed chocolates?

    a) **various**   b) **identical**   c) **born**   d) **hatch**

4. Which word might we use to mean a *particular* flavor?

    a) **familiar**   b) **common**   c) **obvious**   d) **specific**

5. Which word relates to learning about someone or something?

    a) **refer**   b) **acquaint**   c) **bear**   d) **distinct**

EXERCISE C   Circle two words which either are similar or opposite meanings. Write the letter **S** if they are similar, or **0** if they are opposite. *Optional:* Use a thesaurus for more synonyms and antonyms for Exercise A words.

1. familiar   hatch   obvious   refer   _____

2. common   leveret   various   ordinary   _____

3. obvious   young   unclear   hare   _____

4. aerie   bear   familiar   unknown   _____

5. hatch   direct   refer   kitten   _____

EXERCISE D

Write on the line the correct list word to complete each sentence.

When Sarah saw the _ faces from church, she felt more comfortable.	1.
The _ belief was that Padre Pio was a saint!	2.
We spotted a bear and her _ while we were hiking.	3.
An _ is the nest of a bird on a cliff or mountaintop.	4.
The little chicks began to _ on Easter morning.	5.
The newborn _ had long, spindly legs as she stood by her mother.	6.
Dad said my rabbit is really a _.	7.
A collie and a poodle are both dogs, but they are quite _.	8.
Sister Miriam said we should _ ourselves with the Little Way of St. Therese.	9.
It is _ that Gracie loves her baby brother, Liam.	10.
Father Walker said he needed a _ time for a special anniversary Mass.	11.
My brother told me to _ to the Bible to read the details about Daniel.	12.
Dad said those rabbits will _ little bunnies very shortly.	13.
The _ twins like to wear matching dresses to church.	14.
The _ colors of the priests' vestments represent the different feasts or seasons.	15.

CROSSWORD PUZZLE

Use the words from this lesson to complete the crossword puzzle.

ACROSS

1 very clear
3 particular
6 known
7 nest of a large bird built on a cliff or a mountain
9 to come out of an egg at birth
11 to become familiar with
13 to direct attention to someone or something
14 an animal that was just born or hatched

DOWN

2 exactly alike
4 usual; ordinary
5 different in kind or sort
6 the young of a horse
8 clearly different
10 animal that looks like a rabbit, but has longer ears and longer legs
12 to give birth

LESSON
18

UNCLE RONALD HAD A FARM

Uncle Ron bought a farm, and the Grover family went to see it. The children had seen many pictures of farm animals. Farm animals were the topic of conversation for the duration of the trip.

"Do all the animals sleep together in a barn?" Dan asked.

Dad informed him that chickens sleep in coops, and horses sleep in stables.

"Where do pigs and rabbits stay?" asked Jane.

"A pig lives in a sty," Dad answered, "but your uncle had to build hutches for the rabbits. During the day, cows, sheep, and goats graze in a pasture, while the horses graze in a paddock."

Excitement increased as they approached the farm.

"This will be quite an adventure," Mom predicted.

EXERCISE A In the reading above, underline the words (or form of the words) that appear in the list below. Write the dictionary definition for the specific part of speech (noun, verb, adjective, or adverb) as used in the reading.

1. topic (n.) _____

2. conversation (n.) _____

3. duration (n.) _____

4. inform (v.) _____

5. coop (n.) _____

6. stable (n.) _____

7. sty (n.) _____

8. hutch (n.) _____

9. graze (v.) _____

10. pasture (n.) _____

11. paddock (n.) _____

12. excitement (n.) _____

13. increase (v.) _____

14. approach (v.) _____

15. predict (v.) _____

EXERCISE B

Circle the correct word.

1. Which activity may happen over the telephone?

   a) **duration**   b) **conversation**   c) **hutch**   d) **coop**

2. Which word is a place that could NOT possibly hold a cow?

   a) **pasture**   b) **stable**   c) **hutch**   d) **paddock**

3. Which word is a place for animals that have only two legs?

   a) **coop**   b) **sty**   c) **topic**   d) **stable**

4. Which word might we use when someone tells us something we did not know?

   a) **excitement**   b) **approach**   c) **conversation**   d) **inform**

5. Which word means *for as long as something takes*?

   a) **excitement**   b) **conversation**   c) **duration**   d) **topic**

EXERCISE C

Circle two words which either are similar or opposite meanings. Write the letter **S** if they are similar, or **O** if they are opposite. *Optional:* Use a thesaurus for more synonyms and antonyms for Exercise A words.

1. coop   excitement   boredom   duration   _____

2. approach   graze   predict   arrive   _____

3. increase   predict   inform   decrease   _____

4. idea   farm   topic   paddock   _____

5. predict   guess   inform   graze   _____

EXERCISE D

Write on the line the correct list word to complete each sentence.

The _ of my paragraph is the miracles of Jesus.	1. _____
We had a rather excited _ about the parish baseball team!	2. _____
Father Carlton's sermon was to _ us about the sacrament of Penance.	3. _____
The young man in the Bible ate and slept with the pigs in their _.	4. _____
Dad built a new chicken _ for the nuns at that convent.	5. _____
Harry built a rabbit _ about two feet off the ground.	6. _____
Baby Jesus was born in a _ in Bethlehem.	7. _____
The shepherds sent the sheep to _ as they followed the angel to the stable.	8. _____
It was a short distance from the _ to the stable.	9. _____
Some travelers visiting Jesus in the stable put their horses in the _.	10. _____
There was much _ among the shepherds as they knelt before Jesus.	11. _____
Several prophets were inspired to _ the coming of the Savior.	12. _____
The lepers wanted to_ Jesus to be cured of their disease.	13. _____
For the _ of the novena, Mom said we should attend daily Mass.	14. _____
If we _ our daily prayer time, we can become closer to Jesus and Mary.	15. _____

CROSSWORD PUZZLE Use the words from this lesson to complete the crossword puzzle.

ACROSS

3 to feed upon growing grass

6 area of grass where cows graze

7 grassy area where horses graze

8 to come closer

12 talk between two or more people

14 pen in which rabbits are kept

15 building in which chickens are kept

DOWN

1 to grow

2 to guess something before it actually happens

4 strong feeling of joy and expectation

5 pen in which pigs are kept

9 period of time that something lasts

10 building in which horses and cows are kept

11 subject; main idea

13 to give some facts or details about something

LESSON 19

E - I - E - I - OH - OH

Lively conversation at the dinner table was in progress. Laura was telling her experience of the day.

"Hens do not smile in their coops the way they do in our reading books," she related. "They have sharp beaks which are menacing. They have severe beady eyes which appear to threaten me. As Aunt Grace gathered eggs, I had to clutch her belt."

"I wanted to milk a cow," Anne said. "Then I spied a cow as big as our van! I would not dare approach it!"

Dave added, "I had planned to be the Lone Ranger. We had a promising start as I climbed up and straddled my horse Silver. Then Silver broke into a canter heading toward a low fence. As I suspected, Silver jumped. Silver went up and over, and the Lone Ranger went down and under!"

Laughing hard, Mom reminded us, "I knew this visit would be an adventure!"

EXERCISE A In the reading above, underline the words (or form of the words) that appear in the list below. Write the dictionary definition for the specific part of speech (noun, verb, adjective, or adverb) as used in the reading.

1. lively (adj.) _____

2. progress (n.) _____

3. relate (v.) _____

4. menace (v.) _____

5. severe (adj.) _____

6. beady (adj.) _____

7. threaten (v.) _____

8. gather (v.) _____

9. clutch (v.) _____

10. spy (v.) _____

11. dare (v.) _____

12. promising (adj.) _____

13. straddle (v.) _____

14. canter (n.) _____

15. suspect (v.) _____

EXERCISE B Circle the correct word.

1. Which action can we do with a fence or a chair?

   a) straddle   b) canter   c) chime in   d) relate

2. Which word may describe someone who has musical talent?

   a) menace   b) severe   c) promising   d) relate

3. Which word might we use when we see a friend in a crowd?

   a) suspect   b) clutch   c) gather   d) spy

4. Which word refers to a type of run?

   a) dare   b) relate   c) straddle   d) canter

5. Which word might we use when we think something is about to happen?

   a) suspect   b) progress   c) gather   d) dare

EXERCISE C Circle two words which either are similar or opposite meanings. Write the letter **S** if they are similar, or **O** if they are opposite. *Optional:* Use a thesaurus for more synonyms and antonyms for Exercise A words.

1. clutch   straddle   gather   collect   _____

2. promising   dull   lively   beady   _____

3. relate   suspect   tell   dare   _____

4. menace   threaten   beady   lively   _____

5. dare   clutch   straddle   release   _____

EXERCISE D Write on the line the correct list word to complete each sentence.

The bears started to _ the campers and the campsite.	1. _____
Tommy's chance for winning a scholarship to the seminary looks very _.	2. _____
The _ look on the policeman's face warned Jenny that something was wrong.	3. _____
The stern detective's _ eyes saw everything at a glance!	4. _____
The square dancers were swinging this way and that to follow the _ music.	5. _____
The approaching storms _ the start of the rosary rally.	6. _____
Every morning, I _ my scapular and kiss it.	7. _____
The horse's _ caused a cloud of dust.	8. _____
Jesus started to_ His apostles around Him to give His Sermon on the Mount.	9. _____
Jesus often would _ a story or a parable to explain a lesson.	10. _____
None of the apostles could _ that Judas would betray Jesus.	11. _____
"You are too late; the May Crowning is already in _ ."	12. _____
When a senator will not make a commitment, he is known to "_ the fence."	13. _____
Brave Air Force pilots _ to fly the supersonic planes, even to 540 miles per hour!	14. _____
As Nick looked around the tree, he could _ the running deer.	15. _____

CROSSWORD PUZZLE

Use the words from this lesson to complete the crossword puzzle.

ACROSS

1   to spot; to catch sight of
5   strict; serious
8   small, round, and shiny
9   to be a possible danger
10 to sit with one leg on one side and one leg on the other side of something
13 to collect items
14 to show as a possible danger; to threaten

DOWN

1   to have a vague idea about something for which we do not yet have proof
2   full of energy
3   development; advancement
4   likely to lead to successful results
6   to hold onto firmly
7   a horse's run at a slow gallop
11 to tell the details of an event or story
12 to have the courage or boldness to do something

LESSON 20

MAKING A MEMORY

Baby Alice's bonnet has a fringe and showy ruffles. Her dainty appearance draws affection

from everyone. Grandpa decides to be playful by placing the bonnet on his head. At this comical sight,

Grandma begins to cackle gleefully. When the laughter subsides, Grandma whips the bonnet from

Grandpa's head. She places it on the head of Noodle, our poodle. Noodle twirls with frantic delight. Then

Noodle poses so that everyone may admire her. Guffaws burst from the children! This event will become

a memory that our family will relate for years to come!

EXERCISE A In the reading above, underline the words (or form of the words) that appear in the list below. Write the dictionary definition for the specific part of speech (noun, verb, adjective, or adverb) as used in the reading.

1. fringe (n.) _____

2. showy (adj.) _____

3. ruffle (n.) _____

4. dainty (adj.) _____

5. appearance (n.) _____

6. draw (v.) _____

7. comical (adj.) _____

8. cackle (v.) _____

9. subside (v.) _____

10. frantic (adj.) _____

11. delight (n.) _____

12. pose (v.) _____

13. guffaw (n.) _____

14. burst (v.) _____

15. memory (n.) _____

EXERCISE B   Circle the correct word.

1. Which word is something we may find on the hem of a dress?

    a) bonnet   b) appearance   c) guffaw   d) ruffle

2. Which verb says what we do when someone takes our picture?

    a) draw   b) subside   c) pose   d) burst

3. Which word may describe a tiny, thin seashell?

    a) dainty   b) frantic   c) comical   d) fringe

4. Which word relates to very loud laughter?

    a) guffaw   b) memory   c) ruffle   d) appearance

5. Which word refers to remembering an event?

    a) joke   b) memory   c) bonnet   d) ruffle

EXERCISE C   Circle two words which either are similar or opposite meanings. Write the letter **S** if they are similar, or **O** if they are opposite. *Optional:* Use a thesaurus for more synonyms and antonyms for Exercise A words.

1. subside   grow   cackle   pose   _____

2. comical   witty   noisy   fancy   _____

3. affection   delight   pain   grandfather   _____

4. showy   funny   noisy   plain   _____

5. draw   cackle   burst   explode   _____

EXERCISE D

Write on the line the correct list word to complete each sentence.

With great _, the elderly residents of St. James Home sang Christmas carols.	1. _____
Mom made special pink curtains with a wide _ for the girls' bedroom.	2. _____
The nuns made a _ of golden thread for the altar cloth.	3. _____
The small, _ Chinese doll wore a dress of green and gold.	4. _____
They carried a large bouquet of _ flowers to place at Mary's shrine.	5. _____
The _ clown performed to raise money for St. Anne's Hospital.	6. _____
The Confirmation class wanted to _ with the bishop for a photograph.	7. _____
"Because of His miracles, Jesus began to _ huge crowds to follow Him."	8. _____
After telling the funny story, Grandpa gave a loud laugh, a _ , which surprised Mom!	9. _____
As the teens performed at the nursing home, some residents started to _ with great glee!	10. _____
Noah sent the dove outside the Ark to see if the water started to _.	11. _____
The children _ with screams of delight to see the monkey.	12. _____
The student's _ was so good, he remembered every line of the novena prayer.	13. _____
Father said that in a crisis, instead of being _, we should calmly pray to Jesus.	14. _____
The Blessed Mother's _ surprised the three children.	15. _____

Use the words from this lesson to complete the crossword puzzle.

ACROSS

1   to laugh sharply and noisily

4   delicate

5   very loud laughter

7   a pleated or gathered strip of fabric used
    to decorate a piece of cloth

10 to bring out; to produce

12 funny; witty

13 to sit or stand still in such a way as to be
    noticed or admired

14 pleasure

15 very fancy

DOWN

2   the way someone or something looks

3   a trimming or border of hanging threads
    on a piece of cloth

6   to become less

8   something remembered from the past

9   excited

11 to suddenly show expression

LESSON 21

LIMERICKS ARE FUN

Quick Rick explored a dark cave
And encountered a problem quite grave.
He stepped on a bear
That did hibernate there!
I'm glad Rick was more quick than brave.

This five-line poem is called a limerick. Even though a limerick is usually silly in content, one must be clever to write a true limerick. The first two lines and the last line of the verse must all rhyme. The two middle lines rhyme with each other. Another characteristic of a limerick is its rhythm, which imitates the beat of a bouncing ball. Finally, the concluding line is a witty comment.

EXERCISE A In the reading above, underline the words (or form of the words) that appear in the list below. Write the dictionary definition for the specific part of speech (noun, verb, adjective, or adverb) as used in the reading.

1. explore (v.) _____

2. encounter (v.) _____

3. grave (adj.) _____

4. hibernate (v.) _____

5. poem (n.) _____

6. limerick (n.) _____

7. silly (adj.) _____

8. clever (adj.) _____

9. verse (n.) _____

10. rhyme (v.) _____

11. characteristic (n.) _____

12. rhythm (n.) _____

13. imitate (v.) _____

14. conclude (v.) _____

15. witty (adj.) _____

EXERCISE B   Circle the correct word.

1. Which word means *to discover by chance*?

   a) explore   b) imitate   c) encounter   d) hibernate

2. Which word means *serious*?

   a) silly   b) clever   c) witty   d) grave

3. Which word does NOT relate to a limerick?

   a) rhyme   b) imitate   c) rhythm   d) silly

4. Which word suggests sleeping uninterrupted for a long time?

   a) hibernate   b) imitate   c) explore   d) encounter

5. Which word means *to carefully go through or search something*?

   a) encounter   b) explore   c) limerick   d) imitate

EXERCISE C   Circle two words which either are similar or opposite meanings. Write the letter **S** if they are similar, or **O** if they are opposite. *Optional:* Use a thesaurus for more synonyms and antonyms for Exercise A words.

1. amusing   verse   witty   imitate   _____

2. rhythm   rhyme   content   beat   _____

3. silly   conclude   grave   exploring   _____

4. conclude   begin   imitate   encounter   _____

5. clever   characteristic   poem   quality   _____

EXERCISE D

Write on the line the correct list word to complete each sentence.

Some animals _ or sleep during the winter months.	1.
Dad said we should try not to ask _ questions but to think before we ask.	2.
For a sin to be mortal, it must be very serious, that is, of a very _ matter.	3.
Charlene made everyone laugh with her clever and _ comments!	4.
Michael wrote that strange but funny rhyming _.	5.
When Ann read the poem out loud, the _ was obvious.	6.
Sister Margaret said our book report should be about the saint's main _.	7.
"Try to _ St. Therese by offering up little sacrifices for the holy souls!"	8.
"When we _ a difficult person, try to smile and be friendly."	9.
The last _ of the poem is about the beauty of a waterfall.	10.
The altar boys decided to _ the Shenandoah Caverns with their dads.	11.
Mom read us the _ "Lovely Lady Dressed in Blue."	12.
A _ author writes surprise endings to his stories.	13.
Mom asked me to find words which _ with my spelling words.	14.
Mom said to _ my paragraph with a personal comment.	15.

CROSSWORD PUZZLE

Use the words from this lesson to complete the crossword puzzle.

ACROSS

1 to end; to finish

3 to sound alike

5 to pass the winter resting or sleeping

9 lacking seriousness or importance

11 a rhyming piece of writing that tells a story or expresses a feeling

12 cleverly amusing or funny

13 special quality that makes something different from others

14 having a quick and imaginative mind

15 writing in which words are arranged to create a rhythm, a pattern of sounds

DOWN

2 a five-line poem that is usually humorous

4 serious

6 to come upon someone or something unexpectedly

7 to search through something

8 a flow of rising and falling sounds in a poem; the beat of a poem

10 to sound, act, or look like someone or something

LESSON 22

MEET THE SMITHS

Before there were machines, people needed to make their own items out of metals. Some people did this for a living; they were called smiths. They specialized in the craft of shaping metals into useful items. This required a great deal of patience, skill, and precision. Smiths needed to use certain standards. Only an experienced coppersmith, for example, could make a lovely brooch from rough copper. It was a challenging undertaking for a silversmith or a tinsmith to temper metal into forms suitable for cups, dishes, utensils, and weapons. To temper, the metal needed to be heated, shaped, and cooled. In modern days, some people express their talents in the ancient art of shaping metals. Goldsmiths, for example, express their talent in the form of fine jewelry. The best smiths of today continue to uphold the same standards as the best smiths of long ago.

EXERCISE A In the reading above, underline the words (or form of the words) that appear in the list below. Write the dictionary definition for the specific part of speech (noun, verb, adjective, or adverb) as used in the reading.

1. smith (n.) _____

2. specialize (v.) _____

3. craft (n.) _____

4. require (v.) _____

5. skill (n.) _____

6. precision (n.) _____

7. standard (n.) _____

8. experienced (adj.) _____

9. brooch (n.) _____

10. undertaking (n.) _____

11. suitable (adj.) _____

12. utensil (n.) _____

13. express (v.) _____

14. ancient (adj.) _____

15. uphold (v.) _____

EXERCISE B   Circle the correct word.

1.   Which word describes someone who has worked at a skill for years?

   a)   ancient   b)   suitable   c)   experienced   d)   standard

2.   Which word means *a talent in a particular area*?

   a)   skill   b)   brooch   c)   standard   d)   undertaking

3.   Which word means *to need something in particular*?

   a)   suitable   b)   express   c)   precise   d)   require

4.   Which word describes tribes of the Old Testament?

   a)   suitable   b)   ancient   c)   smith   d)   standard

5.   Which word includes such items as spoons, pots, and pans?

   a)   smith   b)   craft   c)   utensils   d)   undertaking

EXERCISE C   Circle two words which either are similar or opposite meanings. Write the letter **S** if they are similar, or **O** if they are opposite. *Optional:* Use a thesaurus for more synonyms and antonyms for Exercise A words.

1.   precision   exactness   undertaking   ancient   _____

2.   ancient   experienced   modern   suitable   _____

3.   utensil   brooch   craft   skill   _____

4.   project   undertaking   express   uphold   _____

5.   craftsman   standard   smith   suitable   _____

EXERCISE D   Write on the line the correct list word to complete each sentence.

Mom said that only a white dress is _ for my First Holy Communion.	1. _____
The rose bushes _ good soil, sunlight, and water.	2. _____
In _ Egypt, the Israelites were forced to live in slavery.	3. _____
Sister said that we must have a high _ for being honest and telling the truth.	4. _____
My grandfather was a _ in a small town in Montana.	5. _____
Betty wanted to _ her love for the Blessed Mother by painting a picture of her.	6. _____
Cutting the marble for the altar rail required great _ .	7. _____
The silver _ worn by mother contained a tiny painting of Our Lady of Lourdes.	8. _____
Our pastor wants to _ the bishop's regulations for proper dress at Mass.	9. _____
With great _, the young man juggled with swords at the church festival.	10. _____
My electric can opener is my favorite kitchen _ .	11. _____
As an _ gardener, Judy took care of the beautiful church gardens.	12. _____
The college professor wants to _ in Catholic Church history.	13. _____
The teenagers took on quite an _ when they worked on the pro-life campaign.	14. _____
Barbara worked to perfect her _ of restoring old church statues.	15. _____

CROSSWORD PUZZLE

Use the words from this lesson to complete the crossword puzzle.

ACROSS

4   being fit or right for a certain use

9   very old

10   ability that comes from training or practice

11   a worker in metals

13   to state; to represent by a sign or symbol

14   to support

15   exactness

DOWN

1   skill in making things especially with the hands

2   to limit oneself to one business or subject

3   an ornamental pin worn on clothing

5   an attempt at an accomplishment

6   made skillful or wise through practice

7   a tool or container usually used in a kitchen

8   something set up as a rule or model

12   to have a need for something

LESSON 23

THE PLEDGE OF ALLEGIANCE

"I pledge allegiance to the flag of the United States of America, and to the republic for which it stands, one nation, under God, indivisible, with liberty and justice for all."

Francis Bellamy wrote this pledge to America over a century ago, in 1892. He proposed a patriotic ceremony to celebrate the 400th anniversary of the arrival of Christopher Columbus in North America. In 1954, the Knights of Columbus made a petition to Congress to add the words "under God." School children continue to recite the pledge in unison daily. May the pledge endure in this millennium and beyond.

EXERCISE A In the reading above, underline the words (or form of the words) that appear in the list below. Write the dictionary definition for the specific part of speech (noun, verb, adjective, or adverb) as used in the reading.

1. pledge (v.) _____

2. allegiance (n.) _____

3. republic (n.) _____

4. nation (n.) _____

5. indivisible (adj.) _____

6. liberty (n.) _____

7. justice (n.) _____

8. century (n.) _____

9. propose (v.) _____

10. patriotic (adj.) _____

11. ceremony (n.) _____

12. petition (n.) _____

13. recite (v.) _____

14. unison (n.) _____

15. millennium (n.) _____

EXERCISE B

Circle the correct word.

1. Which word can refer to a wedding?

    a)   pledge   b)   ceremony   c)   propose   d)   allegiance

2. Which word means what slaves want?

    a)   republic   b)   century   c)   liberty   d)   unison

3. Which word describes people who recite the Pledge of Allegiance?

    a)   patriotic   b)   allergic   c)   republic   d)   pledge

4. Which word means *present an idea* to someone?

    a)   recite   b)   ceremony   c)   pledge   d)   propose

5. Which word means parishioners say prayers *in one voice*?

    a)   recite   b)   unison   c)   petition   d)   nation

EXERCISE C

Circle two words which either are similar or opposite meanings. Write the letter **S** if they are similar, or **O** if they are opposite. *Optional:* Use a thesaurus for more synonyms and antonyms for Exercise A words.

1. justice   freedom   fairness   petition   _____

2. millennium   fifty years   birthday   1000 years   _____

3. pledge   recite   unison   promise   _____

4. century   breakable   indivisible   petition   _____

5. petition   allegiance   republic   loyalty   _____

EXERCISE D   Write on the line the correct list word to complete each sentence.

The missionary would _ that he will teach the young children about the Faith.	1.
St. Thomas More said his first _ is to God, not to the king.	2.
The United States Constitution proclaims that our country is a _.	3.
_ means equal protection under the law for the rich as well as the poor.	4.
Have you ever attended Seton's graduation _?	5.
One of the greatest gifts a free nation has is _ which must always be protected.	6.
The United States has been a generous _ by giving money and food to the poor.	7.
Very few things in this world are _, that is, not able to be separated or divided.	8.
Our neighbors asked us to sign a _ for the pro-life candidate.	9.
We always sing _ songs when the parade goes by on July 4th.	10.
The mayor will _ a new town budget.	11.
The year 2001 marked the beginning of the second _.	12.
The children will _ the Christmas poem in the Christmas play.	13.
The young children found it difficult to sing together in _.	14.
Automobiles and phones are wonderful inventions of the twentieth _.	15.

CROSSWORD PUZZLE Use the words from this lesson to complete the crossword puzzle.

ACROSS

1 loyalty; faithfulness

4 to promise

5 place where a group of people live under one government

6 period of 1000 years

10 government in which citizens have power and express this power by voting for their representatives

12 recitation of words by a group all together (as one)

13 having love for one's country

14 fairness

15 freedom

DOWN

2 unable to be separated or broken up

3 formal request

7 an act or set of acts to be done on special occasions, such as a holiday or wedding

8 to repeat something from memory

9 to suggest

11 period of one hundred years

LESSON 24

GOOD JOB, ZOE

A screech pierces the sleepy household.

"Come see! Oh, hurry! Come see!" The cry echoes through the house.

The children fly down the stairs lickety-split. They peer into the room.

"Puppies!" one exclaims.

Seven balls of fur squeal, whimper, and squirm near Zoe, their mama. They can scarcely stand on their tiny, wobbly legs.

Finally, Duncan, the puppies' papa, trudges in and pokes his wet nose into Zoe's neck.

"Well done," he seems to tell her.

Quite contented now, he lies down beside his little family.

EXERCISE A In the reading above, underline the words (or form of the words) that appear in the list below. Write the dictionary definition for the specific part of speech (noun, verb, adjective, or adverb) as used in the reading.

1. screech (n.) _____

2. pierce (v.) _____

3. household (n.) _____

4. echo (v.) _____

5. lickety-split (adv.) _____

6. peer (v.) _____

7. exclaim (v.) _____

8. squeal (v.) _____

9. whimper (v.) _____

10. squirm (v.) _____

11. scarcely (adv.) _____

12. wobbly (adj.) _____

13. trudge (v.) _____

14. poke (v.) _____

15. contented (adj.) _____

EXERCISE B

Circle the correct word.

1. Which word does NOT relate to excitement?

   a) screech   b) squeal   c) lickety-split   d) contented

2. Which word involves the eyes?

   a) trudge   b) peer   c) exclaim   d) screech

3. Which word may describe a loose tooth?

   a) scarcely   b) whimper   c) wobbly   d) lickety-split

4. Which word relates to repetition?

   a) echo   b) exclaim   c) screech   d) poke

5. Which word involves the feet?

   a) pierce   b) peer   c) exclaim   d) trudge

EXERCISE C

Circle two words which either are similar or opposite meanings. Write the letter **S** if they are similar, or **O** if they are opposite. *Optional:* Use a thesaurus for more synonyms and antonyms for Exercise A words.

1. squeal   yelp   puppy   squirm   _____

2. scarcely   wobbly   squeal   completely   _____

3. household   peer   family   pierce   _____

4. squirm   poke   shout   screech   _____

5. walking   whimper   cry   wobbly   _____

EXERCISE D   Write on the line the correct list word to complete each sentence.

The singing of the Catholic nuns seemed to _ across the valley.	1. _____
Because he was late for dinner, Jimmy ran _ all the way home.	2. _____
The children of Fatima let out a _ as they see the vision of hell.	3. _____
The fire alarms _ the quiet of the night.	4. _____
The weary traveler was _ to return home to his family.	5. _____
After the miracle by St. Francis, the little girl's legs were no longer _.	6. _____
The short man in the tree had to _ through the branches to see Jesus.	7. _____
The soldiers had to _ for miles in the heavy clay soil.	8. _____
St. Peter baptized the whole _ of the prison's jailer.	9. _____
The pigs began to grunt and _ at mealtime.	10. _____
Do not _ your finger into the icing on the cake.	11. _____
As the children began to _ in their seats, Sister Mary led them in saying a rosary.	12. _____
Father Barter had _ begun his homily when the church bell rang.	13. _____
"Lazarus is alive!" the people _.	14. _____
When the light was turned off, the baby began to _ in his crib.	15. _____

CROSSWORD PUZZLE Use the words from this lesson to complete the crossword puzzle.

ACROSS

2 the persons who live as a family in one house

8 to send a sound out and back

10 to penetrate

11 to jab

12 speedily

14 to cry out or speak out suddenly or with strong feeling

DOWN

1 to walk or march steadily but with great effort

3 to make a shrill, high-pitched sound

4 to cry in broken, gasping, or whining sounds

5 shrill, harsh cry

6 barely enough; only just

7 moving or swaying unsteadily

9 satisfied with one's possessions or life

11 to look at carefully or with curiosity

13 to wiggle; to twist about

Answer Key

LESSON 1

Ex. B
1. a) distinguish
2. c) accurate
3. d) insert
4. b) hesitate
5. b) master

Ex. C
1. O – confidence/doubt
2. S – exactly/precisely
3. S – unfamiliar/strange
4. O – urge/discourage
5. O – multiple/single

Ex. D
1. confidence
2. unfamiliar
3. pertain
4. urge
5. Determine
6. hesitate
7. precisely
8. method
9. effective
10. distinguish
11. master
12. insert
13. apply
14. multiple
15. accurate

LESSON 2

Ex. B
1. c) startle
2. d) sheepish
3. b) mislead
4. a) firm
5. b) fetch

Ex. C
1. S – snooze/nap
2. O – fetch/return
3. S – feeble/weak
4. S – object/protest
5. O – mumble/shout

Ex. D
1. brace
2. supreme
3. sheepish
4. snooze
5. mumble
6. fetch
7. giggle
8. firm
9. startle
10. protest
11. feeble
12. pant
13. mislead
14. demand
15. meekly

LESSON 3

Ex. B
1. d) locate
2. b) spine
3. a) table
4. d) assist
5. a) author

Ex. C
1. O – assist/prevent
2. S – likeness/similarity
3. O – locate/lose
4. S – author/writer
5. S – index/list

Ex. D
1. table
2. assist
3. index
4. appear
5. alphabetical
6. identify
7. spine
8. locate
9. chapter
10. section
11. similarity
12. title
13. author

14. address
15. contents

LESSON 4

Ex. B
1. c) yank
2. b) delicate
3. a) spectacular
4. d) chuckle
5. b) dew

Ex. C
1. S – fragile/delicate
2. O- endure/stop
3. S – awe/wonder
4. O – cling/yank
5. O – mistaken/correct

Ex. D
1. delicate
2. chuckle
3. awe
4. filament
5. fragile
6. insist
7. blush
8. yank
9. spectacular
10. dew
11. squat
12. design
13. cling
14. mistaken
15. endure

LESSON 5

Ex. B
1. b) smug
2. c) thoroughly
3. a) frown
4. d) drought
5. a) plod

Ex. C
1. S – rather/somewhat
2. S – branch/bough

3. O – unlucky/fortunate
4. S – previous/preceding
5. S – sow/pig

Ex. D

1. frown
2. plod
3. drought
4. rather
5. sow
6. trough
7. dough
8. furrow
9. smug
10. slough
11. bough
12. fortunate
13. stubborn
14. previous
15. thoroughly

Lesson 6

Ex. B

1. d) cooperate
2. b) harmony
3. a) merchant
4. c) harvest
5. b) furnish

Ex. C

1. S – realize/understand
2. S – rely/depend
3. S – transport/carry
4. S – talent/skill
5. S – live/survive

Ex. D

1. talent
2. cattle
3. merchant
4. cooperate
5. survive
6. realize
7. hide
8. harvest
9. architect
10. harmony
11. furnish
12. transport

13. construction
14. product
15. depend

Lesson 7

Ex. B

1. a) gape
2. c) snatch
3. d) patron
4. b) jolt
5. b) tremendous

Ex. C

1. O – run/saunter
2. S – patron/customer
3. O – gape/glance
4. S – witness/person
5. S – hardly/barely

Ex. D

1. shoplifter
2. gape
3. tuck
4. cautiously
5. saunter
6. witness
7. jolt
8. flicker
9. disbelief
10. snatch
11. patron
12. occupy
13. tremendous
14. hardly
15. glance

Lesson 8

Ex. B

1. b) implore
2. c) shiver
3. c) conceal
4. a) slightly
5. d) amazement

Ex. C

1. O – vigorously/slowly
2. O – hide/emerge
3. S – sway/swing

4. S – brim/edge
5. S – gasp/breathe in

Ex. D

1. brim
2. shiver
3. seedling
4. amazement
5. vigorously
6. clump
7. emerge
8. gasp
9. detect
10. eventually
11. sway
12. slightly
13. implore
14. conceal
15. sprout

Lesson 9

Ex. B

1. d) slump
2. a) slither
3. b) meander
4. d) leap
5. c) slump

Ex. C

1. S – glide/waltz
2. S – leap/jump
3. O – bolt/meander
4. O – strut/slump
5. S – run/scamper

Ex. D

1. nippy
2. slump
3. scamper
4. tumble
5. leap
6. whirl
7. waltz
8. stride
9. meander
10. strut
11. bolt
12. slither
13. glide

14. whip
15. shudder

LESSON 10

Ex. B

1. d) performer
2. b) gleeful
3. c) sweep
4. a) stare
5. a) thrill

Ex. C

1. S – fame/glory
2. S – gracefully/smoothly
3. O – boredom/thrill
4. S – large/gigantic
5. O – fatigue/energy

Ex. D

1. aquarium
2. performer
3. applause
4. boredom
5. dart
6. gracefully
7. gigantic
8. sweep
9. swoop
10. stare
11. thrill
12. fame
13. gleeful
14. fatigue
15. glory

LESSON 11

Ex. B

1. c) groan
2. b) detour
3. d) whoop
4. a) adventurous
5. b) positive

Ex. C

1. S – annual/yearly
2. S – enthusiasm/excitement
3. O – ally/enemy
4. S – solve/answer
5. O – gorgeous/ugly

Ex. D

1. annual
2. destination
3. groan
4. gorgeous
5. adventurous
6. detour
7. whoop
8. positive
9. solve
10. shove
11. suggest
12. ally
13. chorus
14. scenic
15. enthusiasm

LESSON 12

Ex. B

1. b) earn
2. c) aromatic
3. a) substitute
4. c) fond
5. d) scamp

Ex. C

1. S – mischief/trouble
2. S – substitute/replace
3. O – fail/manage
4. O – trot/stand
5. S – type/sort

Ex. D

1. manage
2. mischief
3. trot
4. fond
5. sopping
6. drench
7. sort
8. grin
9. substitute
10. earn
11. aromatic
12. scamp
13. wriggle
14. attempt
15. drool

LESSON 13

Ex. B

1. d) topple
2. b) missile
3. a) powerful
4. c) picture
5. d) yelp

Ex. C

1. S – strike/hit
2. S – surprised/stunned
3. O – flash/hours
4. S – missile/rocket
5. S – throw/shoot

Ex. D

1. picture
2. yank
3. lap
4. topple
5. missile
6. yelp
7. sting
8. upset
9. flash
10. stunned
11. powerful
12. protection
13. fist
14. strike
15. shoot

LESSON 14

Ex. B

1. b) appreciate
2. c) crimson
3. d) spot
4. a) penetrating
5. a) describe

Ex. C

1. O – sunset/dawn
2. O – confusion/understanding
3. S – seem/appear
4. S – opportunity/chance
5. O – giggle/roar

Ex. D

1. jointly
2. dawn

3. appreciate
4. opportunity
5. agree
6. crimson
7. capable
8. bewilder
9. penetrating
10. confusion
11. pipe
12. describe
13. seem
14. spot
15. roar

Lesson 15

Ex. B

1. a) bungle
2. d) amuse
3. b) stammer
4. a) grace
5. c) affectionately

Ex. C

1. O – good-natured/angry
2. S – need/lack
3. O – good luck/misfortune
4. O – moving/boring
5. S – opinion/judgment

Ex. D

1. misfortune
2. moving
3. bungle
4. clumsy
5. dizzy
6. experience
7. affectionately
8. opinion
9. amuse
10. embarrass
11. stammer
12. good-natured
13. lack
14. humor
15. grace

Lesson 16

Ex. B

1. b) scramble
2. a) remarkably
3. d) zealous
4. c) accomplished
5. b) anxious

Ex. C

1. S – yearn/desire
2. S – lively/frisky
3. S – stubby/short
4. S – eager/impatient
5. O – whit/ large amount

Ex. D

1. social
2. yearn
3. drab
4. eager
5. zealous
6. scramble
7. frisky
8. remarkably
9. accomplished
10. keen
11. stubby
12. whit
13. scraps
14. incredible
15. anxious

Lesson 17

Ex. B

1. c) young
2. b) hatch
3. a) various
4. d) specific
5. b) acquaint

Ex. C

1. S – familiar/obvious
2. S – common/ordinary
3. O – obvious/unclear
4. O – familiar/unknown
5. S – direct/refer

Ex. D

1. familiar
2. common

3. young
4. aerie
5. hatch
6. foal
7. hare
8. distinct
9. acquaint
10. obvious
11. specific
12. refer
13. bear
14. identical
15. various

Lesson 18

Ex. B

1. b) conversation
2. c) hutch
3. a) coop
4. d) inform
5. c) duration

Ex. C

1. O – excitement/boredom
2. S – approach/arrive
3. O – increase/decrease
4. S – idea/topic
5. S – predict/guess

Ex. D

1. topic
2. conversation
3. inform
4. sty
5. coop
6. hutch
7. stable
8. graze
9. pasture
10. paddock
11. excitement
12. predict
13. approach
14. duration
15. increase

LESSON 19

Ex. B

1. a) straddle
2. c) promising
3. d) spy
4. d) canter
5. a) suspect

Ex. C

1. S – gather/collect
2. O – dull/lively
3. S – relate/tell
4. S – menace/threaten
5. O – clutch/release

Ex. D

1. menace
2. promising
3. severe
4. beady
5. lively
6. threaten
7. clutch
8. canter
9. gather
10. relate
11. suspect
12. progress
13. straddle
14. dare
15. spy

LESSON 20

Ex. B

1. d) ruffle
2. c) pose
3. a) dainty
4. a) guffaw
5. b) memory

Ex. C

1. O – subside/grow
2. S – comical/witty
3. O – delight/pain
4. O – showy/plain
5. S – burst/explode

Ex. D

1. delight
2. ruffle

3. fringe
4. dainty
5. showy
6. comical
7. pose
8. draw
9. guffaw
10. cackle
11. subside
12. burst
13. memory
14. frantic
15. appearance

LESSON 21

Ex. B

1. c) encounter
2. d) grave
3. b) imitate
4. a) hibernate
5. b) explore

Ex. C

6. S – amusing/witty
7. S – rhythm/beat
8. O – silly/grave
9. O –conclude/begin
10. S – characteristic/quality

Ex. D

1. hibernate
2. silly
3. grave
4. witty
5. limerick
6. rhythm
7. characteristic
8. imitate
9. encounter
10. verse
11. explore
12. poem
13. clever
14. rhyme
15. conclude

LESSON 22

Ex. B

1. c) experienced
2. a) skill
3. d) require
4. b) ancient
5. c) utensils

Ex. C

1. S – precision/exactness
2. O – ancient/modern
3. S – craft/skill
4. S - project/undertaking
5. S – craftsman/smith

Ex. D

1. suitable
2. require
3. ancient
4. standard
5. smith
6. express
7. precision
8. brooch
9. uphold
10. skill
11. utensil
12. experienced
13. specialize
14. undertaking
15. craft

LESSON 23

Ex. B

1. b) ceremony
2. c) liberty
3. a) patriotic
4. d) propose
5. b) unison

Ex. C

1. S – justice/fairness
2. S – millennium/1000 years
3. S – pledge/promise
4. O – breakable/indivisible
5. S – allegiance/loyalty

Ex. D

1. pledge
2. allegiance

3. republic
4. Justice
5. ceremony
6. liberty
7. nation
8. indivisible
9. petition
10. patriotic
11. propose
12. millennium
13. recite
14. unison
15. century

LESSON 24

Ex. B

1. d) contented
2. b) peer
3. c) wobbly

4. a) echo
5. d) trudge

Ex. C

1. S – squeal/yelp
2. O – scarcely/completely
3. S – household/family
4. S – shout/screech
5. S – whimper/cry

Ex. D

1. echo
2. lickety-split
3. screech
4. pierce
5. contented
6. wobbly
7. peer
8. trudge
9. household

10. squeal
11. poke
12. squirm
13. scarcely
14. exclaim
15. whimper

Alphabetical Listing of Words

The number following each word indicates the lesson in which it can be found.

accomplished 16

accurate 1

acquaint 17

address 3

adventurous 11

aerie 17

affectionately 15

agree 14

allegiance 23

ally 11

alphabetical 3

amazement 8

amuse 15

ancient 22

annual 11

anxious 16

appear 3

appearance 20

applause 10

apply 1

appreciate 14

approach 18

aquarium 10

architect 6

aromatic 12

assist 3

attempt 12

author 3

awe 4

beady 19

bear 17

bewilder 14

blush 4

bolt 9

boredom 10

bough 5

brace 2

brim 8

brooch 22

bungle 15

burst 20

cackle 20

canter 19

capable 14

cattle 6

cautiously 7

century 23

ceremony 23

chapter 3

characteristic 21

chorus 11

chuckle 4

clever 21

cling 4

clump 8

clumsy 15

clutch 19

comical 20

common 17

conceal 8

conclude 21

confidence 1

confusion 14

construction 6

contented 24

contents 3

conversation 18

coop 18

cooperate 6

craft 22

crimson 14

dainty 20

dare 19

dart 10

dawn 14

delicate 4

delight 20

demand 2

depend 6

describe 14

design 4

destination 11

detect 8

determine 1

detour 11

dew 4

disbelief 7

distinct 17

distinguish 1

dizzy 15

dough 5

drab 16

draw 20

drench 12

drool 12

drought 5

duration 18

eager 16

earn 12

echo 24

effective 1

embarrass 15

emerge 8

encounter 21

endure 4

enthusiasm 11

eventually 8

excitement 18

exclaim 24

experience 15

experienced 22

explore 21

express 22

fame 10

familiar 17

fatigue 10

feeble 2

fetch 2

filament 4

firm 2

fist 13

flash 13

flicker 7

foal 17

fond 12	hibernate 21	menace 19	poem 21
fortunate 5	hide 6	merchant 6	poke 24
fragile 4	household 24	method 1	pose 20
frantic 20	humor 15	millennium 23	positive 11
fringe 20	hutch 18	mischief 12	powerful 13
frisky 16	identical 17	misfortune 15	precisely 1
frown 5	identify 3	mislead 2	precision 22
furnish 6	imitate 21	missile 13	predict 18
furrow 5	implore 8	mistaken 4	previous 5
gape 7	increase 18	moving 15	product 6
gasp 8	incredible 16	multiple 1	progress 19
gather 19	index 3	mumble 2	promising 19
gigantic 10	indivisible 23	nation 23	propose 23
giggle 2	inform 18	nippy 9	protection 13
glance 7	insert 1	obvious 17	protest 2
gleeful 10	insist 4	occupy 7	rather 5
glide 9	jointly 14	opinion 15	realize 6
glory 10	jolt 7	opportunity 14	recite 23
good-natured 15	justice 23	paddock 18	refer 17
gorgeous 11	keen 16	pant 2	relate 19
grace 15	lack 15	pasture 18	remarkably 16
gracefully 10	lap 13	patriotic 23	republic 23
grave 21	leap 9	patron 7	require 22
graze 18	liberty 23	peer 24	rhyme 21
grin 12	lickety-split 24	penetrating 14	rhythm 21
groan 11	limerick 21	performer 10	roar 14
guffaw 20	lively 19	pertain 1	ruffle 20
hardly 7	locate 3	petition 23	saunter 7
hare 17	manage 12	picture 13	scamp 12
harmony 6	master 1	pierce 24	scamper 9
harvest 6	meander 9	pipe 14	scarcely 24
hatch 17	meekly 2	pledge 23	scenic 11
hesitate 1	memory 20	plod 5	scramble 16

scraps 16

screech 24

section 3

seedling 8

seem 14

severe 19

sheepish 2

shiver 8

shoot 13

shoplifter 7

shove 11

showy 20

shudder 9

silly 21

similarity 3

skill 22

slightly 8

slither 9

slough 5

slump 9

smith 22

smug 5

snatch 7

snooze 2

social 16

solve 11

sopping 12

sort 12

sow 5

specialize 22

specific 17

spectacular 4

spine 3

spot 14

sprout 8

spy 19

squat 4

squeal 24

squirm 24

stable 18

stammer 15

standard 22

stare 10

startle 2

sting 13

straddle 19

stride 9

strike 13

strut 9

stubborn 5

stubby 16

stunned 13

sty 18

subside 20

substitute 12

suggest 11

suitable 22

supreme 2

survive 6

suspect 19

sway 8

sweep 10

swoop 10

table 3

talent 6

thoroughly 5

threaten 19

thrill 10

title 3

topic 18

topple 13

transport 6

tremendous 7

trot 12

trough 5

trudge 24

tuck 7

tumble 9

undertaking 22

unfamiliar 1

unison 23

uphold 22

upset 13

urge 1

utensil 22

various 17

verse 21

vigorously 8

waltz 9

whimper 24

whip 9

whirl 9

whit 16

whoop 11

witness 7

witty 21

wobbly 24

wriggle 12

yank 4, 13

yearn 16

yelp 13

young 17

zealous 16

Like our books?

You might like our program, too. Seton Home Study School offers a full curriculum program for Kindergarten through Twelfth Grade. We include daily lesson plans, answer keys, quarterly tests, and much more. Our staff of teachers and counselors is available to answer questions and offer help. We keep student records and send out diplomas that are backed by our accreditation with the Southern Association of Colleges and Schools and the Commission on International and Transregional Accreditation.

For more information about Seton Home Study School,
please contact our admissions office.

Seton Home Study School
1350 Progress Drive
Front Royal, VA 22630

Phone: 540-636-9990 • Fax: 540-636-1602
Internet: www.setonhome.org • E-mail: info@setonhome.org